STO

DO NOT REMOVE
CARDS FROM POCKET

89-1

THINK about
Poverty in the U.S.

THINK *about*
Poverty in the U.S.

Problems and Policies

*Daniel W. Woods and
John B. Williamson*
The THINK Series

Walker and Company
720 Fifth Ave.
New York City, NY 10019

The THINK Series' Editors: William N. Thorndike Jr.,
Ramsey R. Walker

Stylistic editor: Mary Jo Willy
Fact checker: Catherine Monk
Reading consultants: Anne-Marie Longo, Paula Sable

Jacket design: Joyce C. Weston
Text design: Joyce C. Weston
Photo research: Diane Hamilton
Graphs: Jill Thompson
Jacket illustration: Tom Hughes
Text illustrations: Jeff Danziger
Appendix A written by J. B. Schramm

The editors would like to thank the many teachers, librarians,
and students that assisted in putting together the THINK
Series. It would be impossible to thank everybody; however,
we would especially like to thank the following people: John
Buckey, Betty Carter, Jim Davis, Mike Hartoonian, Tedd Levy,
David Mallery, Mike Printz, Bill Polk, Mary Tabor, Ellen
Ramsey.

First published in the United States of America
in 1988 by the Walker Publishing Company, Inc.

Published simultaneously in Canada by Thomas Allen & Son
Canada, Limited, Markham, Ontario.

Library of Congress Cataloging-in-Publication Data

Woods, Daniel W.
  Think about poverty in the U.S.

  (The Think series)
  Bibliography: p.
  Includes index.
  1. Poor—United States. 2. Poverty. 3. Charities.
4. Public welfare—United States. I. Williamson,
John B. II. Title. III. Series.
HV91.W62 1987   362.5'8'0973   87-25246
ISBN 0-8027-6764-8
ISBN 0-8027-6765-6 (pbk.)

ACKNOWLEDGMENTS

The authors would like to acknowledge research assistance from Larry Snyder and helpful comments from Charlotte Ryan on the issue of health care for the poor.

We also appreciate the care that Barb Smith, Shirley Urban, and Roberta Nerenberg put into the preparation of the manuscript.

CONTENTS

The THINK Series

THINK about
Poverty in the U.S.

1 | Introduction

How can so much poverty exist in a country as wealthy as the United States?

How does poverty affect Americans, especially such groups as the elderly?

Who are the poor in America?

How do we define poverty, and how do we measure it?

Why should you be concerned about this social problem?

How can you, as young Americans, help solve this problem?

An expression one often hears today—in situations where someone is talking too much or perhaps is talking about a topic that seems dry or uninteresting—is "Who cares?" You may look at the title of our book and have a similar reaction.

Who cares?

Why should *you* care? Why should you be concerned about a topic like "the paradox of poverty in America"?

Some of you may have experienced the frustration of not being able to have something you want. But it is one thing to reach into the pockets of your jeans and find that you don't have the money for a second soda, and quite another to worry constantly about where the money for your next meal is coming from, or to have the threat of eviction hanging over your head.

Consider, for example, seventy-year-old Ed MacIntosh, interviewed by Ben Bagdikian in a book called *In the Midst of Plenty*. Mr. MacIntosh's only source of income is a monthly Social Security check. In order to make ends meet one month, he has to sell his television. Bagdikian asks Mr. MacIntosh what things he misses most:

> Things I miss? You haven't got enough paper. . . . My eyes are getting dimmer. I keep having dizzy spells. I keep getting sick to my stomach. . . . I'd like to go to church. I went a year ago. . . . I don't know if I'll be able to go again. . . . Straight up, that is.

How can such things happen in a country which is among the four or five richest nations in the world? This is what we mean by a **paradox**: a statement which does not make logical sense, one which appears to be a total contradiction.

In a country as wealthy as ours, why is a young mother of limited income, whose child is sick, faced with an array of undesirable choices, such as the following? Suppose, for example, that she has three children who are all under five, and one develops an earache. She is immediately confronted with the problem of how to provide for the two healthy children while she seeks help for the one who is ailing. If she is on a tight budget she may not be able to afford a babysitter. Does she then take the three

Figure 1 Poverty in America is frequently found side by side with wealth and plenty.

children on public transportation? Or—if the hospital is not impossibly far away—does she spend money for a cab? This may be money she has to take from her food budget for the month. If she waits, opting to skip the visit to a doctor or hospital, complications may develop. The child may develop a fever and require hospitalization anyway. The mother may find herself accused of neglecting her child.

She may feel that she was balancing various considerations, trying to respond to the child's illness but also being aware of the larger implication for her family finances: how to get through the month. The key question, however, is: why is she placed in this situation at all? Why must she make such choices in a country that is affluent enough to provide adequate medical care for all of its citizens?

HOW DOES POVERTY AFFECT PEOPLE?

Mr. MacIntosh spoke of dizzy spells, of getting sick to his stomach, and of problems with his eyesight. Yet he lacked the resources to get the health care he needed. One of the major effects of being poor in America is limited access to health care. Some scholars speak of a "health gap" separating the poor from those who are more well off. This gap exists from the very beginning of life. If you are born into a poor family, you are less likely to survive to the age of one year than if you are born into a family that is not poor. One key reason is that mothers with limited income are less likely to receive quality prenatal care.

The "health gap" between poor and nonpoor continues—and widens—throughout life. Poor people are less likely to receive immunization against diseases. They are less able to practice preventive measures. They often lack the means to get help when sickness actually strikes.

Chronic health conditions afflict people with low incomes at a rate two to three times higher than those with high incomes. This statement is true not only for the major causes of death like heart disease, cancer, and stroke, but also for such ailments as diabetes, asthma, ulcers, and vision and hearing impairments.

A key issue is the cost of adequate health care. One third of all poor families are not covered by Medicaid, a program financed jointly by state and federal governments and designed to provide medical services for those unable to afford them. Moreover, poor people may have jobs that do not provide sick leave, and this leads to reluctance to take a day off to go to a doctor or dentist.

Few physicians or hospitals are located in poorer areas, and this may make it nearly impossible to reach a doctor. In some rural areas, for example, people have to travel a hundred miles or more in order to get medical help. Transportation difficulties played a part in the decisions of the young mother with a sick child described earlier.

The focus so far has been on the effects of poverty on health. These are by no means the only negative effects of living in poverty. The housing in which poor people live is more likely to be substandard than that of people with higher incomes. Overcrowding, inadequate sanitation, and rats or roaches are problems. Poorer neighborhoods are often shortchanged in city services like garbage collection and police protection. Schools in low-income areas may not have the range of programs or the commitment from school administrators that schools in more affluent areas possess.

Diet among poor people is often inadequate. Forty percent of the poor have serious medical problems because of malnutrition. The popular assumption is that poor people pay less for food than others. In fact, low-income people often pay *more* for food and other staples than shoppers from more affluent areas. They may lack transportation to larger chain stores and end up paying higher prices at small local or convenience stores. Prices for most goods are higher than average, yet the merchandise may be shoddy. In a scam that is fairly common in poorer neighborhoods, used appliances are sometimes passed off as new and resold.

Figure 2   Children playing in a Charlotte, North Carolina, slum. In the distance are the buildings of the financial district.

Clearly a host of problems follows from being poor in America. Who are the poor? Before you read further, you may want to think about your perceptions of the poor. When you think of poverty, what kinds of images come into your mind?

WHO ARE THE POOR?

Who is poor in America? First of all, one person in seven lives below the **poverty line,** a term defined in the next section. This means that thirty-four million people in America are defined as poor. While the overall percentage of poor people in America is 14 percent, poverty affects some groups more than others. For whites, the most recent figure was about 12 percent, or a bit less than the overall average. The figure for blacks below the poverty line was 34 percent, for Hispanics 28 percent. Some people conclude from this that a majority of poor people are black. But blacks make up only 12 percent of the total United States population. While the *rate* of poverty is higher among blacks, whites living below the poverty line comprise 68 percent of all poor people.

Age is also related to chances of being poor. While the proportion of older people living in poverty has declined in the last fifteen years, the proportion of children who are poor has steadily risen in the same period to the present level of 21 percent. Each year, more children live in single-parent families. Such families, if they are headed by women, are more than three times as likely as other families to be below the poverty level.

Geography is also related to poverty. There is considerable variation of income from state to state. In 1986, for example, Connecticut had the highest **per capita income** ($19,208) of any state in America. (Per capita income—literally "by heads"—is figured by taking the total income earned by all residents of a state and dividing it by the number of people in the state.) Mississippi, on the other hand, had a per capita income of $9,552—less than half as much as Connecticut. Even within states there are some striking extremes. The richest county in Alaska (Juneau) had a per capita income five times as large as that of the poorest county (Wade Hampton).

You may have begun to wonder about the relationship between place of birth and chances for success. This is one aspect of what sociologists call **life chances,** or the probability that one will benefit from the opportunities available in a particular society.

Figure 3   On the wrong side of the poverty line, a child's diet may be insufficient and unhealthful.

HOW IS POVERTY MEASURED?

The terms poverty line or poverty level have appeared several times in this chapter. What exactly *is* the poverty line? The following discussion explains these terms and how they are used to define poverty in America.

When the federal government first declared a "War on Poverty" in 1964, an obvious issue which arose was that of counting the poor. Who would receive help from antipoverty programs? How would administrators decide who would get priority attention?

An early measure of poverty—developed by the President's Council of Economic Advisors (CEA) in

1964—defined families with incomes below $3,000 and individuals living alone on less than $1,500 a year as poor. These criteria identified 36 million Americans, or 19 percent of the population, as poor. This measure led to several problems, however. A couple with no children and an income of $2,900 were defined by this measure as poor, while a family of *six* with an income of $200 more ($3,100) were not. Clearly, the second family had a much smaller income per family member.

Other researchers attempted to construct a more practical measure of poverty. To some degree the choice of such a measure is a political one, since **policy** decisions are made on the basis of the criteria chosen. If the measure classifies too many (or too few) as poor, it will not be popular with voters or elected officials.

After examining two measures of poverty developed by the Social Security Administration, President Lyndon B. Johnson's advisors selected the lower of the two income figures and labeled it the poverty line. It is an absolute definition of poverty based on family income. Unlike the CEA measure, it takes into account differences in family size and place of residence. The circumstances of farmers are different from those of city dwellers, for example, in that much of the food consumed may be grown on the farm itself rather than purchased.

In 1984, the poverty line for a nonfarm family of four was $10,609. If this figure seems high, consider an exercise undertaken by Leonard Beeghley in *Living Poorly in America*. Using the 1981 poverty line of $9,287, Beeghley worked out a household budget for a family of two adults and two children. He estimated food expenses at one third of the budget. This amounted to $2.12 per person per day, a figure that would make it very difficult to eat properly. The nonfood budget amounted to $516.17 per month to cover everything else. After money had been allotted to monthly rent ($200), utilities ($100), taxes ($120), and transportation costs ($60), there was only $36.17 left for medical and dental bills, clothing, educational expenses, and entertainment. He concluded that his hypothetical family was not only poor, but "desperate."

WHY BE CONCERNED?

But why should *you* be concerned about poverty? Why should you care?

First of all, poverty is not an abstract issue or one that can be dismissed as irrelevant or boring. Twenty-one of every 100 children in the United States live in a household defined as below the poverty line. Nearly thirteen million kids live in poverty. It is very likely that the lives of people close to you have been or are affected by this social problem. This alone compels a compassionate response.

Secondly, consider for a moment the loss to American society of the full potential and talents of those imprisoned in poverty. How, for example, can a family living in substandard housing, in an apartment that is inadequately heated or not heated at all, and subsisting on a food budget that scarcely allows for one meal a day, mobilize itself to do more than survive? How can children who go to bed hungry and spend a cold and sleepless night do well in school the next day? The loss of talent and energy caused by these conditions is almost incalculable. Such a loss impoverishes American society as well as the persons and families who experience it. It is an example of the **social costs** of poverty in America. Social costs are damages caused to a society by a problem. These can be actual harm, like a crime committed by someone living in poverty, or the loss of something positive, like the loss of the production of workers who are unemployed.

\ A third reason for being concerned about poverty in our nation is its effect upon our political life. An expression Americans frequently use is "can do," implying that every problem has a solution. This is to our credit. But if after twenty-three years of the "War on Poverty," America has still not adequately addressed the problem, what will be the effect on citizens suffering from poverty or those sympathetic to their plight? If our national, state, and local governments are seen by citizens as unable to solve the problem of poverty, it will not be surprising if an increasing number of Americans begin to lose faith in government. They may withdraw from active involvement by not voting or by becoming cynical and apathetic. What will then be the effect on our political life?

¹ Finally, and most importantly, you should be concerned about the paradox of poverty in America because, as President Roosevelt said in his second inaugural address in 1937, it is a "challenge to our democracy." When millions of American citizens are living in conditions which daily force them to make a series of "no-win" choices, this calls into question our commitment to our national ideals, especially the ideal of equality for all.

In this book, we hope to shed some light upon poverty in America and upon related issues. The next chapter will focus on historical background, demonstrating how two very different views of poverty—structural and individualistic—have evolved over the centuries. We will continue this theme (opposing views of poverty) in our third chapter, which focuses on contemporary issues. Another important theme is the relationship between attitudes toward the poor and policies to aid them. Many of these attitudes are evident in the current debate over welfare reform and particularly "workfare" programs of various kinds.

The final chapter tries to predict some of the key issues of the future. Can poverty be eliminated, or is this a goal doomed to failure? What kinds of changes would have to occur in American society for poverty to be reduced to manageable levels?

In approaching the paradox of poverty in an affluent society, we do not propose to give you a boring "academic" view. We aim not only to give you new information and new ideas but also to reach you in such a way that when you read or hear about poor people in America, your response will never be, "Who cares?"

REVIEW QUESTIONS

1. Why is the existence of poverty in America surprising?
2. What are some effects of poverty in the United States? Give examples.

3. Do you know anyone like the elderly Mr. Mac-Intosh?
4. What is the "health gap"? Why does it exist?
5. What groups in American society are most likely to be poor?
6. Can you—using ideas from the book as well as your own—come up with a workable definition of poverty?
7. Why is poverty a problem? What are some drawbacks to American society caused by the continued existence of poverty?
8. Discuss with others some possible solutions to the problem of poverty in the United States. See if you can come up with some new approaches and ideas. Are there ways you can help?

2 Historical Background

How was relief provided to the poor in the first fifteen centuries of European history?

How did attitudes toward the poor change, and how were those changes translated into legislation?

How large a role did the federal government play in relieving poverty during the Hoover Administration? The Roosevelt Administration?

What were the major programs of President Johnson's "War on Poverty"?

How has the perception of government's role in relieving poverty changed in the last twenty years?

In a book of this length, we will not be able to give you a very detailed description of historical efforts to relieve the plight of the poor. But we can at least introduce a few key questions that have recurred over the centuries. Two such questions are: (1) What causes poverty? and (2) What are the best remedies for relieving it?

You will see as you read this chapter that explanations of the causes of poverty are of two major types:

structural or individualistic. **Structural explanations of poverty** look to society in order to account for why people are poor. Such an approach considers factors such as availability of employment opportunities, wage scales, inflation, or discrimination.

Individualistic explanations of poverty, on the other hand, tend to seek the causes of poverty in personal traits or characteristics of the poor. Those who look at poverty in this way ask questions about the motivation of poor people, their persistence in seeking or holding jobs, and their consumption habits.

It may occur to you even from so brief an account that the *policies* (ways of dealing with a social problem) developed by governmental or private bodies would vary considerably as supporters of one or the other view were in the political majority. One might, for example, expect those who subscribe to individualistic explanations of poverty to require people to work if they receive aid. One might expect to find direct aid (such as a guaranteed annual income) supported more often by those who hold a structural view of the reasons for poverty. Of course, explanations of poverty are not either/or propositions; to understand poverty fully, we need to take both individual and structural factors into account.

POOR RELIEF IN THE MEDIEVAL ERA

In the early Christian era, one can identify an attitude (later codified in a twelfth-century document called the *Decretum*) that poverty or need was a result of misfortune. The community of Christians was viewed as having an obligation to aid the needy as an act of justice to the individual suffering from misfortune.

After the decline of the Roman Empire and well into the Middle Ages (approximately 500–1500 A.D.), most of the population of Europe lived in small rural settlements. Persons in need usually depended on family and others in the local community. This was a period in which relief institutions as we know them today did not exist at the national or local level.

As the population increased, however, a more organized system of relief was needed. Monasteries (houses for persons under religious vows) began to serve as agencies of relief, particularly in remote areas. Some of them were expressly organized to help those in need, drawing upon the monastery's income and donations to assist those who came begging. Monks also went out from their monasteries to carry food and provisions to those in need.

By the time of the Middle Ages, hospitals—most of them attached to monasteries or located along main routes of travel—had become major sources of assistance to the needy. Medieval hospitals differed from hospitals today in that they provided a variety of services—housing and caring for weary travelers, orphans, the destitute, and the aged. As they began to appear in cities, some of these institutions were taken over by municipal authorities, the responsibility for the poor thus beginning to shift from religious to governmental control. At the level of the local parish, church relief continued. Since each bishop had the duty to feed the poor within his district, a portion of church revenue was set aside for distribution to the poor.

An effective system of poor relief had been developed largely under church control. The Christian church's theory of the causes of poverty was basically a structural one, in which the poor were held to be victims of circumstance and not to be blamed for their situation. Relief was provided as an act of social justice.

POOR RELIEF IN ENGLAND

This system of poor relief was unable to deal with the growing numbers of destitute, or poverty-stricken, that emerged with the sweeping social, economic, and religious changes in Europe in the fifteenth and sixteenth centuries.

In 1531, the English Parliament passed a bill directing that local officials search out and register destitute persons and assign them areas where they might beg. The bill provided that unauthorized, able-bodied beggars be whipped publicly until the blood ran.

This bill was an important milestone in the history of poor relief. It made a distinction between beggars unable to help themselves and the able-bodied, a distinction similar to the one implicit in modern discussions of the "deserving" and "undeserving" poor. A key element of such distinctions was a judgment as to the cause of poverty. Was it the result of forces beyond the person's control, such as illness or advanced age, and therefore not one's own "fault"? Or was poverty the result of personal shortcomings, such as laziness and—to use a seventeenth-century term—"thriftless" behavior? In the 1601 English Poor Law, the "thriftless" or "able-bodied" poor were categorized as "the vagabond that will abide in no place" and "the idle person."

The 1531 statute seems to us today a mixture of punitive (punishing) and progressive features. The punitive part struck a very different tone from earlier documents like the twelfth-century *Decretum*. It was less compassionate, more likely to blame those living in conditions of poverty. It reflected an attitude very different from the notion of a duty toward the poor, or from the concept of "charity" extended to the less fortunate. Its negative features anticipated attitudes discussed later in this book—attitudes like **Social Darwinism,** or **blaming the victim.** Yet the 1531 statute had positive features as well and was a first step toward a network of relief that was an organized response to poverty.

The Poor Law of 1601 was a similar mixture of the positive and the negative, reflecting perhaps the ambivalence that many feel in the face of poverty. It was in part a response to the near-famine conditions of England in the 1590s. Under the provisions of the 1601 bill, vagrants refusing work could be imprisoned, whipped, branded, stoned, or even put to death.

On the other hand, the Elizabethan Poor Law acknowledged the responsibility of the state in poor relief and defined three major categories of dependents—those "poor by impotency," those "poor by casualty," and "the thriftless poor." The statute directed authorities to take specific measures for each. Children could be apprenticed to anyone willing to take them. The "impotent poor" (aged, lame, blind, or chronically ill) were to be taken care of either in their own homes **(outdoor relief)** or in almshouses, hospitals or "houses of correction" **(indoor relief).**

The able-bodied were to be forced to work or severely punished.

The Poor Law of 1601 also established the "principle of local responsibility." This provided that church wardens from each parish (along with annual appointees) serve as overseers of the poor and as collectors of revenue to carry out the provisions of the act.

While the Poor Law made a distinction between able-bodied and deserving poor, even the latter were not entitled to too much sympathy. The framers of the law believed that if the poor carried the burden of poverty courageously, they would be rewarded in the next world by going to heaven. It was difficult for the Elizabethans—as it still is for us—to entertain the idea that their own society could contribute to causing poverty. The Poor Law of 1601 stood unchallenged for nearly 250 years, with only minor revisions. To some degree its philosophy survives even today.

Between 1760 and 1818, however, poor relief payments in England increased sixfold, while the population only doubled. Taxes increased, and along with them the belief that the poor were not only lazy but were being encouraged by relief measures to increase their numbers. In this climate of opinion, the Poor Laws came under attack from several sources. One source was the "classical economists," who believed that poverty was the "natural state" of the wage-earning classes and that the accumulation of property and wealth by the higher classes in society was a "natural right" not to be interfered with.

With the decline in influence of the old landed aristocracy in many European countries, and the rise to power of the growing middle classes, a new eco-

Figure 4   An elderly woman receives food in a nine-teenth-century poorhouse.

nomic philosophy began to arise: **laissez faire,** or noninterference in economic affairs. Laissez faire involved the assumption that the economy will regulate itself. In somewhat altered form it is still with us today. Such a philosophy opposed any restrictions on trade or industry, and its proponents urged "reform" of "anachronistic" laws. The Poor Laws were regarded as not only outmoded but actually harmful.

An influential figure was Thomas Malthus, whose *Essay on the Principle of Population* was published in 1798. Malthus advocated total abolition of the Poor Law. He argued that it caused overpopulation, lowered wages and living standards, and in general caused more misery than it relieved.

The criticisms of the Poor Law led to the creation of a Royal Poor Law Commission. Most of its members subscribed to a laissez-faire economic philosophy. Its 1834 report contained two provisions immediately enacted into law. The first of these called for a national supervisory body to coordinate and improve poor law services throughout Great Britain. The second reflected a growing trend toward indoor relief; it recommended an end to public assistance for the able-bodied except in public institutions. You will note that the language specifies "able-bodied" persons. But this provision was carried out in such a way that most of those on public relief—including children, the aged, the ill, and the disabled—were deprived of outdoor assistance.

The tone of the report implied that poverty was an individual moral matter, somehow the fault of the impoverished person. The report introduced the **principle of less eligibility.** This guaranteed that "the condition of all welfare recipients, regardless of need or cause, should be worse than that of the lowest-paid self-supporting laborer." The Poor Law Reform Act of 1834 which resulted exemplifies a punitive attitude toward the destitute.

This attitude toward the poor was described by

Figure 5 A school for destitute children in London, showing conditions like those described by Charles Dickens in his novel Oliver Twist.

Charles Dickens in the following passage from his novel *Oliver Twist*, first published in 1838:

> The room in which the boys were fed was a large stone hall, with a copper at one end: out of which the master, dressed in an apron for the purpose, and assisted by one or two women, ladled the gruel at meal-times. Of this festive composition, each boy had one porringer, and no more except on occasions of great public rejoicing, when he had two ounces and a quarter of bread besides. Boys have generally excellent appetites. Oliver Twist and his companions suffered the tortures of slow starvation for three months . . . A council was held, lots were cast who should walk up to the master after supper that evening, and ask for more; and it fell to Oliver Twist.
>
> The evening arrived; the boys took their places.

Oliver was desperate with hunger, and reckless with misery. He rose from the table; and advancing to the master, basin and spoon in hand, said, somewhat alarmed at his own temerity:

"Please, sir, I want some more."

The master was a fat, healthy man; but he turned very pale. He gazed in stupefied astonishment on the small rebel for some seconds; and then clung for support to the copper.

"What!" said the master at length, in a faint voice.

"Please, sir," replied Oliver, "I want some more."

The master aimed a blow at Oliver's head with the ladle; pinioned him in his arms; and shrieked aloud for the beadle.

How different the attitude of the 1834 Poor Law and the master in *Oliver Twist* was from what we have described as that of the early Christian and medieval era, when it was assumed that need arose

Figure 6 When Oliver Twist dared to ask for more food, he was expelled from the orphanage that had cared for him, demonstrating the miserable conditions that existed for poor children in nineteenth-century England.

from misfortune and that society should take the responsibility to alleviate it. We have already suggested one way of looking at the differences between these two views, calling them individualistic explanations and structural explanations. In Chapter Three we will provide more detail. Let us turn now to poverty in the New World.

POVERTY IN AMERICA

Since the early colonists were mainly English, perceptions of the poor paralleled those we have already discussed. The English Poor Law of 1601 set the pattern of relief for the destitute in America as well.

While colonial America did not experience as much poverty as the Old World, poverty was still in evidence. Because of the high mortality rate, children were sometimes left without parents. Others also required assistance: widows, the mentally and physically handicapped, the ill, and the aged.

Since settlements were small and far apart, local officials decided who needed aid and how funds were to be provided. If the community believed that a nonresident was likely to become a public charge, he or she might be "warned out" of the settlement— told to leave.

By the second half of the seventeenth century, settlements had grown to a degree that an approach beyond local aid was needed. In 1647, Rhode Island enacted the first colonial poor law. In 1657, Renssalaerswyck, New York, was the site of the first almshouse for the provision of indoor relief to the poor. Plymouth Colony and Boston established almshouses in 1658 and 1660.

By the end of the seventeenth century, a trend toward centralization in providing poor relief had developed. The major responsibility for aiding the poor had passed from local to larger units of government.

As the population of America, which was still overwhelmingly rural, grew, so did indoor relief. The first "poor farm"—an American adaptation of the workhouse—was established near Philadelphia in 1711. In 1727 in New Orleans, the Ursuline Sisters set up the first orphanage in the American colonies. It housed children whose parents had been killed in an Indian raid. In 1773 in Williamsburg, Virginia, one of the first institutions for the mentally ill, or "lunatics" as they were then bluntly called, was established.

Other kinds of institutions began to appear: juvenile reformatories, institutions for the physically handicapped or the deaf and dumb. Unfortunately, the prevalence of such institutions and the peculiar names of some, such as "House of Refuge for Juvenile

Figure 7   An almshouse in Philadelphia, Pennsylvania, 1799.

Delinquents" or "Society for Inoculating the Poor Gratis," encouraged the notion that those suffering from social problems were somehow radically different—and presumably inferior—from the rest of us.

This **assumption** began to take hold even in a country that was now an independent nation. Post-Revolutionary War America was still very **homogeneous** (composed of inhabitants from similar backgrounds and ethnic groups). When increasing numbers of immigrants from other countries, such as Ireland and Italy, began to arrive in America in the mid- and late-nineteenth century, the descendants of the early settlers were initially skeptical about the new **heterogeneous** society.

Those charged with giving assistance could sometimes barely contain their contempt. They "found it difficult to apply Christian benevolence to . . . ragged, uncouth, 'different' . . . and seemingly immoral newcomers." One of the reasons for this attitude was the popularity of the Protestant **work ethic**, which identified worldly success with heavenly salvation. Another was a deep-seated belief, still widespread today, that everyone can succeed, and that if someone doesn't, it follows that he or she must be at fault.

The notion that the poor are fundamentally different from others was carried to an illogical extreme by the English engineer-turned-social-philosopher Herbert Spencer, who coined the phrase "survival of the fittest." Spencer tried to apply the biological ideas of Charles Darwin to the social environment. Social Darwinists believed that the conflicts between social groups produce a social order that is natural and correct. They felt, therefore, that government should not support education, regulate business or trade, or provide postal or sanitary services. They also believed that government should definitely not be involved in providing assistance to the poor.

Competition was seen as the basic law of life and self-help as the only remedy for poverty. Government intervention was perceived as "artificial" and as an interference with the designs of God. One Social Darwinist went so far as to speak of assistance to the poor as an effort "to prolong the life of the unfit." Such language would be unheard-of today.

Yet negative attitudes toward the poor—and particularly those on welfare—are by no means completely absent from our society even today. For a few minutes, list some of the things you have heard said by friends or acquaintances about the poor, the homeless, "street people," etc. You may be surprised at some of the items you have listed.

What we are trying to emphasize is the degree to which assumptions and attitudes about the poor af-

Figure 8   Social Darwinists believed that the poor were to be ignored in a healthy society.

fect public debate on policies. (An **attitude** is a system of beliefs concerning something, which results in an evaluation of it.) Throughout most of the nineteenth century and the first three decades of the twentieth century in America, attitudes based on individualistic explanations dominated public debate and policy.

One needs to look at the institutions of nineteenth-century America in historical context. They were—however constrained by attitudes like those embodied in Social Darwinism—attempts to respond to the social problems of a nation undergoing rapid change. The population of America rose from five million at the beginning of the century to nearly 76 million by its close. Industrialization, urbanization, and the growing power and influence of business all played a part in attitudes toward the poor and the policies developed to assist them.

One revealing example was the "orphan trains" of Charles Loring Brace, founder and executive director of the New York Children's Aid Society. Faced with the problem of thousands of homeless children wandering the streets of New York, Brace established children's shelters, free reading rooms, and industrial schools. He felt that a key solution lay in transporting vagrant children from the "demoralizing" city to the "more virtuous" rural areas. For twenty-five years "orphan trains" ran, and it is estimated that more than fifty thousand children were placed in private homes, most of them with farmers in the Midwest.

It was a solution both ingenious and naive, and came under criticism even in its own era for failing to investigate the prospective foster parents thoroughly and for allowing some of the children to be exploited as cheap labor. Later studies have found, however,

Figure 9   Poor children on a Salvation Army trip to a rural area, 1904.

that the program was largely successful, especially for the younger children.

It was difficult for institutions like almshouses and poor farms to keep pace with the growing demands upon them. Of particular concern was the treatment of children in increasingly crowded and badly maintained institutions. Separate facilities for children began to multiply, and by 1890 more than six hundred "orphan asylums" were in operation in America. These housed anywhere from fifty to two thousand children each.

Some observers became concerned about conditions in the various nineteenth-century institutions.

Figure 10   The occupants and staff of the Christian Orphans' Home in Holdrege, Nebraska, pictured here in 1896.

Dorothea Dix—a social reformer—took as her special concern the treatment of the insane. She traveled more than sixty thousand miles to inspect jails, prisons, and workhouses in twenty-seven states. Dix managed to persuade Congress to pass a bill setting aside ten million acres of land for the establishment of hospitals for the insane, and 2.5 million acres for institutions for the deaf.

The attempt to involve the federal government on so large a scale in solving social problems was unprecedented. But President Franklin Pierce vetoed the bill in 1854, saying that he could not "find any authority in the Constitution for making the federal government the great almoner (supporter) of public charity throughout the United States." This view prevailed until the New Deal legislation of the 1930s.

Clearly, individualistic views predominated over structural ones, and the federal government was not yet ready to take major responsibility for alleviating social problems like poverty.

Let's flash forward now, to the period just before the Great Depression. A common belief of the time was that the 1920s were "the prosperity decade," and that there was no need to improve the social environment. Speaking in October of 1928, President Herbert Hoover said:

> Our American experiment in human welfare has yielded a degree of well-being unparalleled in all the world. It has come nearer to the abolition of poverty, to the abolition of fear of want, than humanity has ever reached before.

Some signs of economic problems, however, could be recognized as early as 1928. Unemployment, for example, was on the rise. But the kind of thinking exemplified by President Hoover's remarks made it difficult to see this as a structural problem rather than as a set of individual ones. Economic trouble was interpreted as a temporary business downturn. Even when the stock market crashed in October of 1929, President Hoover predicted that there would be an immediate recovery. When this did not happen, he urged businessmen to hold prices and wages firm. As things worsened, Hoover took the position that the economy was undergoing a "healthful deflation."

News of the Depression seldom appeared on the front pages of American newspapers until after 1932. Events like the suicide of a financial speculator or the murder of his starving family by an unemployed worker were still interpreted as personal tragedies rather than failures of the social structure of American institutions.

Meanwhile, unemployment topped four million by January of 1930, reached eight million by the spring of 1931, and two years later was at a staggering twelve million—a third of the entire work force as of the spring of 1933. President Hoover—preoccupied with balancing the budget—rejected the recommendation of his own Emergency Committee for Employment to seek money from the Congress for public works. Instead, in December of 1930 he announced that "the fundamental strength of the nation's economic life is unimpaired."

The real problem was not so much the president as the ideology that had become commonplace in the century prior to the Depression. (An **ideology** is a set of beliefs, attitudes, and opinions, whether tightly or loosely related.) The popular laissez-faire philosophy of the market guaranteed that the federal government would be unable to deal with the structural causes of the Depression unless major political changes occurred.

Because of its belief in individualistic explanations of poverty, the Republican administration of Herbert Hoover was unlikely to undertake large-scale government interventions to try to alleviate the growing economic crisis of 1929–1933. Indeed, in 1931 President Hoover vetoed a bill calling for a $2.6 billion federal public works program, saying that "never before in the nation's entire history has anyone made so dangerous a suggestion."

Not all public officials were opposed to government intervention to relieve the economic crisis, however. In 1931, New York State, on the initiative of Governor

Franklin D. Roosevelt, established an emergency program to supplement local relief funds. By the end of 1932, twenty-three other states had followed suit with similar programs. Aid to jobless citizens "must be extended by government, not as a matter of charity, but as a matter of social duty," Roosevelt told a special session of the New York legislature he had called in August of 1931.

As you might expect, Roosevelt's views had appeal beyond the borders of New York to millions who had begun to look to the federal government as the only institution able to rescue them from economic disaster. In the summer of 1932, Roosevelt won the Democratic nomination for president of the United States, setting the stage for a dramatic political reversal. In the general election, Roosevelt defeated President Hoover by seven million votes, winning 472 of 531 electoral votes. His party, the Democrats, also controlled both houses of Congress.

After taking office on March 4, 1933, President Roosevelt proceeded to act upon the principles he had voiced during the campaign. On March 31, the Civilian Conservation Corps was established, providing jobs in the national forests for 250,000 men at subsistence wages. On May 12, the president signed into law the Federal Emergency Relief Act. This law was tradition-shattering in its transfer of responsibility for large-scale relief from local and state governments to the federal government. Five hundred million dollars of federal funds were distributed under FERA to the states to be used for emergency unemployment relief.

On June 16, the National Industrial Recovery Act passed the Congress. Title II of this statute set up the

Figure 11   Men waiting to receive unemployment compensation at the state employment office, San Francisco, California, 1938.

Public Works Administration (PWA), the purpose of which was to stimulate the economy through the construction of huge public works projects (dams, port facilities, sewage plants, roads, airports, bridges, hospitals) requiring large numbers of workers. Chances are that there is a PWA project fairly close to where you live. On November 8, the Civil Works Administration (CWA) was set up to create jobs for four million workers. Most of the jobs were designed to employ unskilled workers, who were to be paid the minimum wage.

Other programs included the National Youth Administration (NYA), which provided part-time jobs for high school and college students; and the Works Progress Administration (WPA), which provided jobs for the unemployed—including artists, musicians, and scholars. These jobs were suited to the talents and experience of the unemployed.

Before we continue our historical account, it is important to emphasize the major shift in the stance of the federal government, which for the first time in American history officially recognized that poverty could be the result of societal conditions. You may remember the very different outlook of President Pierce in 1854, and the reluctance of President Hoover to depart from an individualistic interpretation of poverty. The evidence of the Depression was increasingly hard to refute, as millions of people began to fall into poverty and individualistic explanations became less and less convincing.

On August 14, 1935, the Social Security Act became law, creating a national system of old-age insurance and also providing federal aid to the states, on a matching basis, for care of women with dependent

Figure 12   Works Progress Administration office in Ohio, 1938. This photograph itself was paid for by the WPA.

children, the crippled, and the blind. **Aid to Families with Dependent Children (AFDC)** is what many Americans rather imprecisely refer to as "welfare" or as a "welfare system." Set up by amendments to the Social Security Act, AFDC allows for payments to families where a dependent child is "deprived of parental support," most often to one-parent families where the father is absent. This provision has led to many of the welfare myths, and problems that we discuss in Chapter 3.

Far from constituting a system, such aid is administered with wide variation from state to state, since the responsibility for determining a needs standard and eligibility for benefits rests with the individual states. In practice, social workers question applicants about the details of their lives.

Of all the new programs, however, it was the Federal Emergency Relief Administration that reached the most destitute. A former employee recalled its spirit in these words: "There was one concern—to distribute as much money as possible, as fast as possible, to as many as possible." By the winter of 1935, twenty million people—one-sixth of the population of the United States at that time—were receiving aid from FERA. A more dramatic change from the philosophy of the previous administration could hardly be imagined. Franklin Roosevelt's philosophy—diametrically opposed to that of Herbert Hoover's—is clear in this excerpt from his Second Inaugural Address (1937):

> Let us ask again: Have we reached the goal of our vision of that fourth day of March 1933? Have we found our happy valley?

I see a great nation, upon a great continent, blessed with a great wealth of natural resources. Its hundred and thirty million people are at peace among themselves; they are making their country a good neighbor among the nations. I see a United States which can demonstrate that, under democratic methods of government, national wealth can be translated into a spreading volume of human comforts hitherto unknown—and the lowest standard of living can be raised far above the level of mere subsistence.

But here is the challenge to our democracy: In this nation I see tens of millions of its citizens—a substantial part of its whole population—who at this very moment are denied the greater part of what the very lowest standards of today call the necessities of life . . .

I see one-third of a nation ill-housed, ill-clad, ill-nourished.

It is not in despair that I paint you that picture. I paint it for you in hope, because the nation, seeing and understanding the injustice in it, proposes to paint it out. We are determined to make every American citizen the subject of his country's interest and concern, and we will never regard any faithful law-abiding groups within our borders as superfluous. The test of our progress is not whether we add more to the abundance of those who have much, it is whether we provide enough for those who have too little.

It would be misleading to leave you with the impression that the programs of the New Deal eliminated poverty in America. They did, however, provide emergency assistance to millions, and may have prevented millions of others from actually falling into poverty. But an indication of the severity of the Depression was that as late as the end of 1938 ten to eleven million Americans were still unemployed. What pumped up the economy and reduced unemployment from eight million to 670,000 between 1940 and 1944 was World War II. In the prosperity that occurred in the postwar period (1946 to 1960), many Americans convinced themselves that poverty was no longer a social problem to contend with and that the "affluent society" was at hand.

Figure 13   An unemployed youth holds his head in frustration, Washington, D.C., 1939.

PERSONALITY PROFILE

DOROTHY DAY

Efforts to relieve poverty have come from private individuals as well as from public institutions. One example is Dorothy Day (1897–1980).

She was in many ways a maverick all her life, "a radical who never got tired." Born in Brooklyn Heights, New York City, she was one of five children of an Episcopalian mother and a Congregationalist father.

At the age of sixteen, she finished high school and won a scholarship to the University of Illinois at Urbana and she had began writing for a local newspaper. Dorothy was appalled by "the ugliness of life in a world which professed itself to be Christian," and she joined the Socialist Party.

When she was eighteen, Dorothy and her family moved to New York City, where she took a job as reporter and columnist with the Socialist *Call* and later wrote for *The Mass* and the *The Liberator*.

After a few false starts, including an attempt at a novel, a trip to Europe, and a stint as a probationary nurse, she entered into a common-law marriage with Forster Batterham. A child, Tamar Teresa, was born in March of 1927, and Day decided she wanted her daughter baptized as a Catholic. She was faced with choosing between the love of her life and a church which frowned upon her common-law marriage, all the more because Batterham was a committed atheist. On December 28, 1927, Dorothy Day entered the Catholic Church. Her radical friends did not approve, nor was she welcomed particularly by Catholics. She supported herself and her daughter by writing.

Five years after her conversion, she met French-born Peter Maurin, who had come up with a philosophy and a program for a "green revolution" uniting scholars and workers in "houses of hospitality" for the poor. Day and Maurin published the first issue of their *Catholic Worker* in May of 1933, selling copies for one cent—the price it still costs 54 years later. The unemployed had begun knocking at the door of the paper, and this was the beginning of St. Joseph's House of Hospitality. During the 1930s, thirty houses of hospitality sprang up across the United States. The number declined with the coming of World War II, when many supporters found the Catholic Worker movement's pacifism unacceptable. Out of a rented building at 175 Chrystie Street, Day and her staff, all living in voluntary poverty, served warm meals and provided a used clothes dispensary for free.

In 1973—at the age of seventy-six—Day still found the energy to plan a shelter for "old women put out of hospitals to actually live in the streets." By 1976 it was opened, ready for use. Day's last major speaking appearance was in August of 1976, in Philadelphia. She reminded her audience that it was the anniversary of Hiroshima, saying that God "gave us life. . . . But we have given the world instruments of death of inconceivable magnitude."

On November 29, 1980—three weeks after her eighty-third birthday—Dorothy Day died. An hour before her funeral on December 2, a diverse crowd of onlookers began to assemble in the street before the Nativity Catholic Church. When Cardinal Terence Cooke met the body at the church door to bless it, a mentally disturbed man pushed his way through the crowd and peered at the coffin while bending over it.

"No one interfered," William Miller writes in his biography of Dorothy Day, "because . . . it was in such as this man that Dorothy had seen the face of God."

"The mystery of the poor is this," Dorothy Day once wrote, "that they are Jesus, and what you do for them you do to him."

A parallel could be drawn between the 1920s and the period after World War II. In both eras, America was considered so prosperous that poverty was not a problem. In 1962, however, a young writer named Michael Harrington published *The Other America: Poverty in the United States.* In this book, Harrington spoke of the "invisible" poor, whom it takes "an effort of the intellect and will even to see." He estimated their number at forty to fifty million, arguing that because they were aged or very young, or lived in areas the middle class avoided, or were politically inactive the rest of America found it easy to ignore their existence.

One of President John F. Kennedy's advisors passed the book on to the president. Harrington was invited to join a task force working on the concept of a "War on Poverty." The principle of the federal government allying itself with those in need was hardly in question anymore, thirty years after Roosevelt's first administration and decades after the inception of New Deal programs. Rather, it had become a question of what exactly the government should do— not whether it had a responsibility in the matter of alleviating poverty.

Then—in November of 1963—President Kennedy was assassinated. The new president, Lyndon B.

Johnson, took as one of his mandates the pursuit of President Kennedy's antipoverty initiatives. On March 16, 1964, he delivered a speech to the Congress calling for a national War on Poverty, reaffirming the responsibility of the federal government in relieving the plight of the poor and proposing an array of programs to solve the problem:

> We are the citizens of the richest and most fortunate nation in the history of the world.
>
> One hundred and eighty years ago we were a small country struggling for survival on the margin of a hostile land.
>
> Today we have established a civilization of free men which spans an entire continent.
>
> With the growth of our country has come opportunity for people—opportunity to educate our children, to use our energies in productive work, to increase our leisure—opportunity for almost every American to hope that through work and talent he could create a better life for himself and his family.
>
> The path forward has not been an easy one.
>
> But we have never lost sight of our goal—an America in which every citizen shares all the opportunities of his society, in which every man has a chance to advance his welfare to the limit of his capacities.
>
> We have come a long way toward this goal.
>
> We still have a long way to go.
>
> The distance which remains is the measure of the great unfinished work of our society.
>
> To finish that work I have called for a national war on poverty. Our objective—total victory. . . .
>
> The war on poverty is not a struggle simply to

support people, to make them dependent on the generosity of others.

It is a struggle to give people a chance.

It is an effort to allow them to develop and use their capacities, as we have been allowed to develop and use ours, so that they can share, as others share, in the promise of this nation.

We do this, first of all, because it is right that we should. . . .

Because it is right, because it is wise, and because, for the first time in our history, it is possible to conquer poverty, I submit, for the consideration of the Congress, the Economic Opportunity Act of 1964.

The act does not merely expand old programs or improve what is already being done. It charts a new course. It strikes at the causes, not just the consequences of poverty. It can be a milestone in our 180-year search for a better life for our people. . . .

Many programs familiar to us today were proposed in this address by President Johnson and subsequently passed by the Congress. The Work-Study Program, for example, designed to stimulate the part-time employment of financially needy college and junior college students, still exists, with the federal government paying up to 80 percent of the students' earnings. Upward Bound focuses on secondary school students who have college potential but inadequate high school preparation. To improve their chances for college admission, Upward Bound provides six- to eight-week precollege summer programs and academic year follow-up activities like group and individual tutoring.

For preschool children, the Economic Opportunity

Act of 1965 established Head Start, a program designed to provide poor children with experiences and resources that will enable them to compete on a more equal basis with other students when they actually begin school.

The programs we have described are educational. Other important programs started under President Johnson include VISTA and the Job Corps. One indication of the impact of the War on Poverty programs is that nearly every city or town with a significant poverty problem now has a local community action agency, charged with the responsibility of coordinating assistance to the poor. The way in which we conceive of and talk about poverty in America has been permanently affected by the federal interventions of the War on Poverty.

Figure 14   A VISTA volunteer with underprivileged children in St. Petersburg, Florida, 1965.

*Figure 15 A Job Corps volunteer training unem-
ployed youths in New York City, 1967.*

In the mid-1970s, however, criticism of federal antipoverty efforts increased. President Nixon began to
appoint agency heads whose task was to dismantle
the very programs they were charged with administering. This was especially ironic in view of the fact
that U.S. Bureau of the Census figures showed a
steady decline in both number of poor and percent of
poor in the total population in the period from 1965
through 1973. The 1965 figures were 33.2 million poor
comprising 17.3 percent of the total population; for
1973, the figures were 23.0 million and 11.1 percent.

In fairness to Nixon, however, it must be pointed
out that a program that would have involved a significant redistribution of income in America almost
came to pass in his first administration. This was the
Family Assistance Plan of 1969, the core of which was

a guaranteed annual income for all citizens, a truly unprecedented notion to Americans. A key dilemma was the "notch," or the point at which to set the FAP benefit so as to provide an adequate income yet encourage recipients to enter the work force. Rising unemployment levels eventually eroded the political support for the Family Assistance Plan.

In the late 1970s, criticisms of a "welfare state" began to multiply, and Ronald Reagan was elected president in 1980 on a platform (a declaration of principles and policies) a key part of which was to reverse or cut back expenses for social programs. In the 1980s the intervention of the government as an ally of the poor has once again become a hotly contested issue.

REVIEW QUESTIONS

1. Describe briefly the attitude toward poverty of the early Christian church.
2. Why did church institutions cease being the primary providers of assistance to the poor?
3. Describe some of the features of laws concerning poor relief passed by the English Parliament in 1531, 1601, and 1834.
4. How were attitudes toward the poor changing between the sixteenth and the eighteenth century? What were some of the reasons for these changes?
5. What does the excerpt from *Oliver Twist* suggest about attitudes toward the poor in the mid-nineteenth century?

6. In America, what effects did massive immigration have upon public perceptions of the poor?
7. Can you define Social Darwinism and describe its implications for assistance of the poor?
8. How did President Hoover deal with the Depression? What were some of the beliefs in his ideology that may have affected his response to this crisis?
9. How did President Roosevelt's beliefs and policies differ from those of President Hoover? In particular, how did they differ concerning the role of the federal government?
10. Describe some of the programs passed by the Congress during President Roosevelt's first administration. What were they designed to do?
11. Describe some of the programs proposed by President Johnson and passed by Congress as part of the "War on Poverty."
12. Has the public perception of the role of government in relieving poverty changed in the last fifteen years? How?

3 | Contemporary Debate

How has the distribution of poverty changed over the last two decades?

What is a stereotype? In what ways do some Americans stereotype the poor?

What is "The American Dream"? The "work ethic"? How do these conceptions affect attitudes toward the poor?

What is meant by a "culture of poverty"?

What are some reforms that have been proposed to improve welfare?

Poverty still has a grip on American society despite the efforts of the New Deal, the War on Poverty, and other programs. Poverty persists, but the poor themselves have changed: there is an alarming percentage of children who are poor, and a growing number of poor people who hold jobs.

This chapter will consider two explanations for poverty: the individualistic "culture of poverty" theory and the "situational" theory, which emphasizes the structural causes of poverty. The chapter will end with a close look at the hotly debated topic of welfare reform.

THE CHANGING COMPOSITION OF THE POOR IN AMERICA

It is worth highlighting the changes in the distribution of the poor over the last two decades. While the situation of the aged has improved somewhat during this period, the situation of the young has become markedly worse. In the period 1968–1983, even as the number of children in the United States *dropped* by 9 million, the number of poor children *increased* by 3 million, to a total of 13.8 million children living in poverty in America. According to a congressional study, one-sixth of all white children, one-third of all Hispanic children, and half of all black children live below the poverty line. The National Advisory Committee on Economic Opportunity calls growth in poverty among the very young "one of the major social disasters" of recent times.

Many of the children classified as poor live in households headed by women, and the Committee observes that nearly one family in three headed by women is poor. The corresponding figure for families headed by men is one in eighteen. In fact, "there are now more poor in female-headed households than in those headed by males for the first time since the data have been gathered." A startling fact is that a third of single mothers who had children under six and who worked full time at some point during the year were poor. Cuts in social programs have made the situation even more critical.

Certain groups are especially vulnerable to poverty—for example, the children of migrant workers. Hundreds of thousands of these children work twelve- to fourteen-hour days, seven days a week. They are constantly exposed to pesticides, leading to frequent illness and sometimes even death. Because they follow the crops, they are prevented from establishing roots in any one community. Many become apathetic and depressed. Seldom do they get a chance to attend school. If they do, it is a matter of weeks before they are on the move again, with no chance for continuity in their schooling. Unless major change occurs, the future of migrant workers' children is bleak.

ATTITUDES TOWARD THE POOR

Some Americans hold negative attitudes toward particular groups in our society. A one-sided and exaggerated view of a group is called a **stereotype**, a kind of "picture in the head" that is fixed and resistant to change. Even the receipt of new information may not alter the stereotype. If, for example, a person holding stereotyped opinions assumes that all Italians love opera, you may volunteer the fact that you are Italian and are not an opera fan. The person who stereotypes may very well respond, "Well, you're not like the rest of them," thus managing to retain the stereotype even in the face of contrary evidence.

The poor—especially those among them who are welfare recipients—are often the victims of stereotypical thinking. Elliot Liebow's *Tally's Corner* can be used to introduce the issues of attitudes and beliefs about the poor.

Liebow describes a pickup truck driving slowly down a street. The driver calls out to a man sitting on a porch, asking if he wants a day's work. The man shakes his head—no. The truck drives on, to a cluster of five men at a take-out restaurant. They also say no.

Figure 16   A Texan migrant worker in a California migrant camp, during peach season 1935. Life remains difficult for many migrant workers.

As the truck makes its way up and down the streets, an occasional man climbs into the back of the truck. Starting and stopping, the truck finally disappears.

Liebow goes on to offer some explanations. Has a "labor scavenger" been rebuffed? Are the men who refused lazy and irresponsible? Or is what we have observed more complex?

It proves to be a weekday morning. Most of the men the driver sees already have jobs. Since they are neither working nor sleeping, they have come out on the street to escape their rooms or apartments. Some work Saturdays and are off on this weekday. Some work for stores that do not open until ten o'clock. Some are construction workers and have come back from the job site because the weather is too cold to pour concrete. Each has his own story, and an outside perspective cannot fully understand the scene unless more information is presented.

This anecdote forces us to look at some of the attitudes we may harbor toward others of different backgrounds or economic circumstances. You have no doubt overheard such attitudes expressed by acquaintances or people in your own neighborhoods.

Recent research in the area of attitudes and beliefs about the poor revealed some surprising conclusions. In one study, 375 men and women in the Boston area were asked a series of questions to discover how well informed they were on a number of factual issues relating to welfare. Participants were asked, for example, "What percent of total welfare recipients are able-bodied, unemployed males?" The actual percentages at the time of the study were:

Children	55.5%
Mothers	18.6%
Aged	15.6%
Blind and Disabled	9.4%
Able-bodied Adult Males	0.9%
	100.0%

The correct answer to the question would have been "one percent." Yet the average response was an astounding 37 percent! Many people clearly believed, wrongly, that a very high percentage of welfare recipients were capable of working. These misconceptions affect the public discussion over poverty and what to do about it.

Another question asked was, "How many children under age eighteen are there in the average AFDC [Aid to Families with Dependent Children] family?" At the time of the study, the average figure for both the United States and Massachusetts was 2.6. The average of the replies was 4.8, again indicating a serious misconception. Respondents overestimated the number of children by 85 percent.

What was most surprising was that such misconceptions were not limited to middle-class respondents, but were believed by the poor themselves.

It is quite possible, then, that many of the poor have **internalized** attitudes toward their own situation that reflect prevailing **values** of American society. One common value is the emphasis upon the **work ethic** in American society.

Some beliefs connected to the work ethic are that (1) each person should work hard and compete with others; (2) that such effort should result in success;

(3) that because of equal opportunity, success actually does result; and (4) that failure to succeed is the fault of the individual and an indication of character flaws.

The first three of these constitute what some would call "The American Dream." Such beliefs have inspired millions of immigrants to come to America and build a new life. Millions have, in fact, done so. Public figures like Governor Mario Cuomo of New York and Governor Michael Dukakis of Massachusetts have spoken openly of the hard work and achievements of their immigrant ancestors.

You have no doubt heard parents and teachers stress the importance of applying yourself and working hard in order to achieve your goals. This is good advice. A problem with the values of the work ethic arises when we seek to account for those in American society who, by any definition of success, are simply not "making it."

Some Americans assume that "street people" do not want to work, that they are "lazy." This is an outlook which looks solely to individual shortcomings and alleged character flaws to explain poverty, ignoring features of the social structure, such as shifts in employment needs and economic downturns. It is, in short, an incomplete explanation of the causes of poverty. Poverty is a complex issue that defies such simple answers.

CAUSES OF POVERTY

Why *do* some people end up at the bottom of American society? What causes poverty? There has never

Figure 17   Homeless people huddling together during the winter in Washington, D.C., 1984.

Figure 18   Some people see individual characteristics, such as laziness, as causes of poverty. Poverty, however, is a complex problem that requires a more complete explanation.

been a shortage of explanations for the existence of poverty.

One of the most famous and controversial of theories about poverty is Oscar Lewis' notion of a "culture of poverty." In 1956, Lewis arrived in Mexico City to study the Casa Grande, a large one-story slum tenement housing seven hundred people. He became very friendly with a fifty-year-old man and his three adult children, all of whom had grown up in a one-room apartment in the Casa Grande. Lewis spent hundreds of hours interviewing the members of this family, and this material—edited and interpreted—became *The Children of Sanchez* (1961), a very influential and widely read book among social scientists.

From his work in the field, Lewis came to feel that he had isolated key features of a **culture of poverty.** Some of the traits Lewis identified among the poor were a trend toward female- or mother-centered families; lack of privacy; and strong feelings of helplessness, dependency, or inferiority. A key implication of this notion is that poverty is passed on by parents to their children.

Lewis was an **anthropologist,** a student of the cultural development, customs, and beliefs of social groups. With its emphasis on observations in the field, Lewis' theory is an example of a **cultural approach to poverty,** one which emphasizes the values and behavior of the poor themselves as the primary cause of continued poverty.

The problem with such an approach is that it focuses attention on presumed characteristics of the poor and overlooks features of the society which may contribute to poverty. It becomes too easy to say,

"Look at these people. See how they live? No wonder they're poor."

William Ryan refers to this tendency as "trying to transform the poor." He argues that such "efforts could not work and did not work. . . . A real war on poverty cannot choose the poor as its targets." It is Ryan who recognized and labeled the process of *blaming the victim,* a convenient designation for the negative attitudes some Americans hold toward the poor.

Ryan's book, *Blaming the Victim,* explains how "blaming the victim" can be applied to almost every social problem. Do people have medical problems? It must be their "fault" for not obtaining proper health information. Are they living in substandard housing? If so, they must be "Southern rural migrants" not yet adjusted to urban life. For almost every problem, there is an "explanation" that basically ends up saying that victims of various problems cause their own troubles. Such "explanations" too easily relieve other people from any responsibility for solving the problem of poverty.

A second approach to explaining the causes of poverty is the **situational approach to poverty,** which views the behavior of the poor as specific adaptations, often creative, to features of the environment, such as low income. In this view, feelings of helplessness, for example, would be regarded as a realistic response to lack of power in the larger society.

Criticisms of Lewis are frequent among those who adopt the situational approach. One critic—Charles Valentine—has argued that many of the "class distinctive traits" identified by Lewis are not cultural patterns inherited and passed on from generation to generation, but rather the product of external conditions. He regards many of these patterns as creative adaptations to living in poverty. An example of this would be trading food stamps with a neighbor in exchange for babysitting services.

The differences between cultural and situational theorists have deep roots. One's view of the reasons why people are poor is closely related to one's view of the world, of human nature—in short, to one's *ideology*. The conflict between cultural and situational theorists is at one level a conflict between those who take the view that poor people are somehow personally responsible for their condition and those who assert that structural and environmental forces are the primary causes of poverty. Situational theorists do not totally reject the notion of a culture of poverty. They say, however, that cultural explanations of poverty are incomplete if they leave out the larger social structure and its impact upon the poor.

WELFARE REFORM

If there is any one issue that will trigger some of the negative attitudes we have described above, it is welfare. You may have already heard remarks from neighbors or acquaintances about welfare "bums," "lazy" recipients who should get out and work, or "cheats" who are "ripping off the taxpayers." These perceptions are stereotypes, but they die hard, even in the face of solid data to the contrary. Leonard Goodwin, for example, in *Do the Poor Want to Work?* found no differences between poor and nonpoor when it came to ambitions and desire to work. And in *Subordinating the Poor*, Joe R. Feagin asserts that prosecutions for welfare fraud (the receipt of welfare benefits by unqualified people) comprise less than one percent of all welfare cases. Yet the stereotypes linger.

One reason, for example, that it is hard for a welfare recipient to get off welfare is that in many states income made from an outside job may be counted against recipients and cause them to be ineligible for further benefits. It is a cruel bind to be in, for if a person decides to forgo work and remain in the situation which most benefits his or her family, he or she is then subject to being viewed by some as a "chiseler."

To say that attitudes about welfare recipients are often stereotypical, however, is not at all the same thing as saying that no problems exist with welfare in its present form. After years of disagreement, politicians of both parties seem finally to have reached a consensus on the need for welfare reform. *Time* magazine ran a lead story on "Fixing Welfare" in its issue of February 16, 1987. Earlier in the same month, Senator Edward M. Kennedy introduced a bill addressing the issue of welfare reform.

Senator Kennedy's bill, called JEDI, or Jobs for Employable Dependent Individuals, provides for the payment of bonuses to states that do well in the training and employment of long-term welfare recipients. These bonuses would be based on the savings to the federal government produced by state efforts. The name of Senator Kennedy's bill—Jobs for Employable *Dependent* Individuals—provides a clue to understanding a debate that has continued over the last twenty-five years.

Often, when public officials with different views

are debating poverty policy, they are so intent on their own positions that they ignore the views of others. If the primary goal of the person proposing a policy is to reduce poverty to negligible levels, then a strategy like the guaranteed income approach (as in the Family Assistance Plan proposed by President Nixon in 1969) is probably the best one. The "trade-off" is continued dependency for large numbers of Americans.

If, on the other hand, the primary goal of the reformer is to reduce dependency, to get people off of welfare, there may be some merit to an approach like **workfare,** in which the recipient of assistance is required to work. The most difficult task of all is to reduce *both* poverty and dependency at the same time.

At the state level, efforts similar to Senator Kennedy's proposal have taken place. These reform efforts are a response to the number of families that receive Aid to Families with Dependent Children. This figure had reached 3.9 million families by 1981. In the late 1980s it has dropped somewhat, perhaps as a result of the Reagan Administration's prodding of states to tighten their eligibility rules.

Some thirty-five states have considered work requirements for welfare recipients in the last six years. In 1982, San Diego County undertook a study of seven thousand AFDC recipients and found that 70 percent looked forward to coming to their work assignments. Sixty percent felt that their work experiences would help them to get better jobs in the future.

A criticism that has been made of "workfare" job search and work requirement programs is that the

Figure 19 A worker examines a list of welfare recipients in New York City.

job skills provided in many training programs are rudimentary, and therefore the jobs they may lead to are dead-end. Some advocates of workfare would argue, on the other hand, that the kind of job is less important than the training and message that a work requirement sends to recipients and nonrecipients alike: that income is the result of labor, and that this exchange should not stop simply because one is receiving government assistance. The assumption is that this social message will encourage individuals to take steps to become less dependent.

PERSONALITY PROFILE

Daniel Patrick Moynihan

Almost certain to be in the center of any debate over social issues in the last twenty-five years is Daniel Patrick Moynihan, United States Senator from New York and former Director of the Harvard–MIT Joint Center for Urban Studies.

It was Daniel Patrick Moynihan—then a presidential assistant for urban affairs—who pushed for a welfare reform package that included a Family Assistance Plan. The rejection of President Nixon's proposal is described in Moynihan's *The Politics of a Guaranteed Income* (1973).

Born in Tulsa, Oklahoma, on March 16, 1927, Moynihan was the oldest of three children. When he was about six months old, his parents moved to New York City, where his father worked as an advertising copywriter for RKO Films. Although the family lived fairly comfortably at first, Pat's father fell into debt, began to drink heavily, and deserted his family in the mid-1930s. Margaret Moynihan and her children lived in various cold-water flats, and for a time they went on welfare.

Moynihan was educated in public and parochial schools, finishing first in the graduating class of 1943 from Benjamin Franklin High School in Harlem. Assuming that he could not afford college, he took a job as a longshoreman. In 1944, he enlisted in the Navy, serving as a gunnery officer. Discharged in 1947, he tended bar for a year in his mother's saloon, and then he resumed his college studies, receiving a B.A.

from Tufts in 1948 and an M.A. in 1949 from Tufts' Fletcher School of Law and Diplomacy.

In 1953, he became involved in Robert F. Wagner's campaign for mayor of New York, and a year later in W. Averell Harriman's campaign for governor. From 1955 through 1960, he held a succession of state posts in New York. In addition to his political activity, he lectured at several local colleges, became an assistant professor of political science at Syracuse University and began contributing articles to the *Reporter*.

During John F. Kennedy's campaign for President, Moynihan wrote position papers on urban problems for him. In 1963, he was named assistant secretary of labor, becoming the youngest subcabinet member in the Kennedy Administration.

Affiliated with the Joint Center for Urban Studies since 1960, Moynihan coauthored *Beyond the Melting Pot* with Nathan Glazer in 1963. In *The Negro Family: A Case for National Action* (1965), which came to be known as "The Moynihan Report," he argued that the instability of black family life—the result of centuries of discrimination—was a major factor in the social disadvantages suffered by black Americans. The report was criticized by several civil rights leaders, and Moynihan responded to the attacks in an article in *Commentary* (February 1967).

As a professor of education and urban politics at Harvard's Kennedy School of Government, he turned his attention to federal antipoverty programs, authoring another controversial book, *Maximum Feasible Misunderstanding: Community Action in the War on Poverty* (1969). He also edited two collections of articles: *On Understanding Poverty* (1969) and *Toward a National Urban Policy* (1970).

From 1973 to 1975 he was United States Ambassador to India; and after he wrote an article criticizing American diplomacy, he was appointed by President Ford as ambassador to the United Nations. After a stormy eight-month stint, he resigned in February of 1976.

He is currently serving as U.S. Senator from New York. Concerned about the emergence of an "underclass" trapped in poverty, Moynihan has tried to highlight the issue. He feels that government policies have in part created a decline in two-parent families, and he urges the adoption of a national family policy. He has set forth these ideas in his book, *Family and Nation* (1986).

Even though the welfare reform efforts that have been described in this chapter are structural in that they are attempts to correct flaws in the structure of welfare programs, they are not structural in another sense. They fail to take into account what is going on in the larger society, especially in the American economy. In several studies, the state of the economy has been shown to relate directly to the numbers of Americans falling below the poverty line.

Part of the attraction of workfare programs is that they appeal to the millions of Americans who believe in the individualistic explanation of poverty. They appeal to those who believe that poverty is caused by individual failures and that if the poor develop new skills and attitudes they will succeed.

While there may be some truth to this view, it ignores altogether such structural components of poverty as racial and sexual discrimination and differences in the distribution of resources in American society. The next section discusses a major element of the social structure: the American economy and its relation to poverty in our nation.

THE ECONOMY, STRUCTURAL UNEMPLOYMENT, AND THE WORKING POOR

In talking about workfare and "welfare to work" programs, we have tried to raise the issue of the economy and its relation to increased poverty in the 1980s. A pertinent question is, "Of what use is it to train welfare recipients for jobs which may prove to be low-paying, dead-end jobs in which they may be trapped for the next ten or twenty years—or even for the rest of their working lives?"

Two observations are important to note here. First of all, poverty is by no means limited to welfare recipients. Three million Americans who work year-round are still poor. Furthermore, if we consider the 22.2 million poor who are fifteen years of age or older, more than nine million of them work for some part of the year. These are the **working poor.** Clearly, living in poverty cannot be equated simply with living on welfare.

Secondly, the changing American economy has a dramatic impact on millions of Americans, and not merely upon those defined officially as poor. This is especially the case when people are thrown out of work by such occurrences as plant shutdowns. M. Harvey Brenner of Johns Hopkins University has calculated the indirect social costs of a 1 percent increase in the unemployment rate, sustained over six years.

Such an increase is associated with the following indirect social costs:

- *37,000 deaths*
- *920 suicides*
- *650 homicides*
- *4000 state mental hospital admissions, and*
- *3300 state prison admissions.*

These social costs are a burden which falls on not only the "official poor," but on millions who do not meet the technical definition of poverty, and on their families, extended families, and friends. There are probably few Americans not touched in one way or another by the continued existence of poverty.

The existence of the working poor is a particularly disturbing kind of poverty, for it calls into question many of our most cherished ideals, such as the emphasis on work as a means of getting ahead. In short, it calls into question part of what Americans have come to call "The American Dream." Many of those who continue to work and yet are not experiencing success come to blame themselves, which adds to their burden

It is important to take a look at the American economy and the changes that have taken place in the last two decades. It is also important to identify the trends which are affecting millions of Americans every day.

A term that is relevant here is **structural unemployment**, which is unemployment caused by changes in the occupational structure. Examples are the shift from heavy to light industry, the shift from manufacturing to service occupations, and the growing number of computer-related, "high-tech" jobs. These changes make it difficult for many workers to retain their old jobs or be retrained for newer ones.

Michael Harrington describes workers displaced from their original jobs as "skidding" from job to job; some finding new work but at lower rates of pay, on the average at salaries that are only 61 percent of what they formerly earned.

In addition to the loss of income the displaced worker must contend with, there is also the loss of self-esteem associated with moving from a job that one feels comfortable with to one that involves new and unfamiliar tasks.

The general shift from "heavy" to "light" industry is called **deindustrialization.** One expert describes the impact upon American workers in devastating terms, citing thirty-eight million jobs in basic industry lost to deindustrialization in the 1970s alone. Perhaps never before in the nation's history have there been such rapid changes in the workplace. It will take imagination and commitment on the part of government and business to address the consequences of these social changes.

As suggested earlier, the issue of poverty cannot be separated from the condition of the American economy. As unemployment goes up, so does poverty. Since 1979, the unemployment rate has generally exceeded 7 percent, and the number of poor people has risen dramatically, from twenty-seven to thirty-four million.

About eight million people in the United States are currently looking for a job and cannot find employment. One million job seekers have given up looking altogether. This is the case despite the creation of twenty million new jobs since 1970. Clearly, there is

Figure 20   A welfare recipient working in return for his check in Salt Lake City, Utah.

_Figure 21 The closing of the U.S. Steel plant in
Chicago, Illinois, in 1984 caused thousands of workers
to lose their jobs._

not a good "fit" between the skills of the unemployed
and the skills required for job openings.

The issues we have highlighted—structural unemployment and deindustrialization—need to be taken
into account in evaluating training or retraining programs for both the working poor and welfare recipients. What such programs can accomplish is

limited by the constraints of a changing economy. Programs like workfare may run the risk of training welfare recipients for an employment structure in need of redesigning. The debate over the solution to the problems surrounding the issue of welfare again points to a recurring theme: the differences between structural and individualistic explanations of poverty and the policy implications of each view.

REVIEW QUESTIONS

1. What are some stereotypes that are held about the poor? What does the evidence actually say concerning these stereotypes?
2. What are four key beliefs that are part of the "work ethic"?
3. Give examples of how attitudes toward the poor are affected by belief in "The American Dream."
4. What are two major approaches to explaining why poverty occurs? How do they differ?
5. What are some flaws in the present system of welfare assistance?
6. Describe some approaches to welfare reform.
7. What is "structural unemployment"?
8. Define the "working poor."
9. What are the advantages of "workfare" or "welfare to work" programs? What are some criticisms of such programs?
10. What is the relation between unemployment and poverty?

4 Future Outlook

Is the elimination of poverty a realistic goal?

How committed is our society to eliminating poverty?

Why is unemployment a key factor in the existence of poverty?

How have the kinds of jobs available in America changed over the last twenty years?

How does the continued existence of poverty raise questions about our commitment to American ideals?

The estimated number of Americans living in poverty in 1964 was thirty-six million. In 1986—twenty-two years after President Johnson declared the "War on Poverty"—the figure was thirty-four million. Although individuals and families have been assisted, clearly the dream of eliminating poverty in the United States has not been realized. But why is this so? Why do we still have the paradox of poverty in an affluent society?

CAN POVERTY BE ELIMINATED?

Michael Harrington, author of *The Other America*, claims that the War on Poverty was never given a chance to work, that it never reached the takeoff point necessary to the success of a federal program. The reason, according to Harrington, was the Vietnam War, which siphoned off funds that would otherwise have been spent on domestic programs.

If Harrington is right, the War on Poverty failed because funds that might have been used to support it were diverted to support a war abroad. Harrington's explanation assumes that the commitment to eliminate poverty was at least present, even if funding proved to be inadequate.

Many people would of course reject the contention that antipoverty programs were inadequately funded. Some argue that hundreds of billions of dollars have already been spent on the poor in America, a transfer of income that is unprecedented in history. Have the results justified the expenditures? Many liberals would say yes, pointing to such things as the improved condition of the elderly. Many conservatives would say no, arguing that dependency on government has increased, and that we now have second- and even third-generation poverty within families.

In a thought-provoking article, sociologist Herbert Gans offers an explanation for the continued existence of poverty that is far more disturbing. Gans' interpretation is a **functional analysis.** It assumes, in short, that if poverty continues to exist in America, it must be serving some functions for those who are not poor. In this view, the commitment to eliminate poverty is clearly *not* present.

What are some of these functions? Gans groups them into economic, social, and political functions. It is the six social functions of the poor, especially "status functions," that are the most disturbing of all. A key function is that the poor serve as a "measuring rod" for others in society. Americans need to know where they "stand." As long as there are poor people at the bottom, others can feel confident about their position in society. What Gans is saying, in effect, is that poverty survives in America because many Americans need a class of people to whom they can feel superior.

An even uglier aspect of these status considerations can be related to some of the attitudes we have identified in the previous chapter. According to Gans, the poor may serve as negative examples for those who wish to justify values like hard work, honesty, or thrift. It becomes easy for some to point the finger at the poor and accuse them of laziness, dishonesty, or excessive spending. Their failure to succeed thus demonstrates the worth of the accepted values.

While we find Gans's analysis interesting, particularly in its emphasis upon the relationship between public attitudes and policy, we cannot accept it as an explanation of the failure to eliminate poverty in the United States. It is useful in highlighting the attitudes held by some Americans, but as a serious analysis of the reasons poverty still persists, it is far too limited.

While we do not presume that we can offer solutions to the problems of poverty in America, we may be able to trace certain trends and give you a sense of possible alternatives.

POSSIBLE SOLUTIONS

Most observers agree that providing more jobs is a desirable policy goal in solving the problem of poverty. The Catholic bishops of the United States, in their pastoral letter on the economy, "recommend that the fiscal and monetary policies of the nation . . . should be coordinated so as to achieve the goal of full employment."

Senator Paul Simon of Illinois has proposed a Guaranteed Job Opportunities Program that would put the poor to work on projects to be chosen by regional councils. Workers would be paid the minimum wage, or 10 percent more than welfare payments or unemployment compensation to work a four-day week. On the fifth day, they would be expected to look for jobs in the private sector. It is a program reminiscent of the New Deal's WPA (Works Progress Administration). It should be pointed out, perhaps, that someone working a full forty-hour week at the minimum wage of $3.35 would make $6,968 for the year. This would be $3,641 below the poverty line of $10,609 for a family of four. If a thirty-two-hour work week is assumed, annual income at the minimum wage would be $5,574, or 53 percent of poverty level income for a family of four. Clearly, such a program is not a long-term solution to the problem of poverty in America.

One way to reframe the problem is to look at it as figuring out a way to create better jobs, not dead-end ones, in the private sector for those who are currently unemployed. Nor is this only a domestic problem. Increasingly, American corporations manufacture their products overseas. This displaces American workers who might otherwise do the assembly work.

Jobs are being created daily, but they are increasingly in the service or "high-tech" sectors. Without extensive retraining of workers, these jobs will not replace positions lost to workers in heavy industry.

Many such jobs require technical training for even entry-level openings.

Journalist Richard Louv cites a powerful statistic: that 46 percent of the recently unemployed were blue-collar workers, while 26 percent were white-collar. This was true despite the fact that white-collar workers outnumbered blue-collar workers by a margin of five to three.

Given a continuation of these trends, what does the future hold? Louv paints a pessimistic picture. The old jobs and roles, he says, are gone forever. The options left to displaced workers without extensive retraining are jobs as janitors, clerks, fast food workers. He sees a workforce that is increasingly separated into unskilled and highly skilled workers.

If Louv's projections are on the mark, they have unsettling consequences. His predictions suggest that we are moving ever more swiftly toward a two-class society, one in which the "haves" and the "have nots" eye each other with mutual suspicion, and the paradox of poverty amid affluence continues, or even worsens.

Some of the signs of an increasingly polarized society are already apparent. If poverty increases among certain groups—families with female heads of household, Hispanics, blacks, children—while other groups such as young urban professionals become more and more affluent, we run the risk of even greater inequalities in our society. Already the resources of surburban school systems are far better than those of most urban and rural school systems, and the gap seems to be widening. What this means is that even at the elementary school level, those already advantaged will have access to resources like personal computers that less advantaged city and rural children will not have, thus increasing the competitive edge of the wealthier systems. (Some efforts are underway to provide less affluent school systems with additional financial assistance.)

We are a nation that professes a deep-rooted belief in equality; yet at the present time inequality seems to be on the rise in our society.

It is important to realize that many of the conditions we have described in this book are the result of decisions made by human beings in positions of power and influence. Poverty is not a part of the "natural order of things," as some would argue.

Consider, for example, the decisions made by many American businesses to use foreign labor, thus eliminating jobs that could be held by American workers. Consider, also, the shift away from an economy based on manufacturing to a service economy, and the increase in automation. These are all a part of a natural evolution and have helped the American economy to advance. A modern economy strives to provide less expensive products and better services. There are, however, often human costs to these changes. Many people have lost their jobs or been unable to find any suitable employment at all. Some corporations, however, are already beginning to make efforts to reconsider or delay plant closings and to retrain displaced workers.

Americans are perhaps the most idealistic people in the world. When we set out to *eliminate* poverty, filled with our "can do" philosophy, our expectations were excessive. The prevailing belief of the time was that one could solve a problem if one were willing to spend enough money. It is not surprising that in his

Figure 22   Plant closings, a direct result of deindus-trialization, put many qualified people out of work.

campaign for President in 1980, Ronald Reagan was able to make an issue of excessive federal spending, or that—once in office—he was able to gain congressional support for cutting back on food stamps and other social programs.

Congress balked, however, at eliminating or significantly reducing Social Security, which is the biggest income-transfer program of all, comprising one-fifth of the federal budget. This is a measure of the degree to which the principle of federal support of individual citizens is accepted. Other examples of government-funded programs that are widely accepted are Medicare and Medicaid. Programs like these, along with food stamps, prevent large numbers of Americans from falling into poverty.

Is it possible, however, to *eliminate* poverty in America? A key question for us is: are we willing to pay the political costs? To eliminate *poverty*, the strategy that probably makes most sense is some form of guaranteed annual income. But often there is another priority as well: to eliminate *dependency* upon public assistance. These two goals are probably contradictory. We cannot eliminate poverty and dependency at the same time.

If the primary goal is to eliminate dependency, this may mean learning to live with a certain amount of poverty. If our primary goal is to *reduce* poverty to a manageable size, we will probably increase dependency, at least in the short run.

In any event, public officials of opposing views need to thrash out a realistic agenda for the reduction of poverty and inequality in America. There are already some encouraging signs that this kind of dialogue is beginning to become more widespread.

We would like to close our book with a direct appeal to you, our readers. There is an alarming tendency in some young people today to make decisions solely on the basis of personal gain.

You will be the decision-makers of tomorrow. You will be in a position not long from now—as citizens and consumers—to consider the human cost of key decisions, and then to act accordingly. We have tried to show that the present state of America is the result of decisions made by human beings—some good decisions, some bad. We hope that this book has given you some things to think about.

Some people will tell you that social programs are necessary because without them the potential for social unrest increases. While this may be so, this is not the best reason for supporting a goal like the reduction of poverty.

Inequality is inconsistent with the principles upon which our nation was founded. It is a contradiction of our belief in liberty and justice for all when children go to bed hungry at night, when people cannot afford to go to the doctor, when some do not have even a roof over their heads.

It is time to do away with the paradox of thirty-four million people living in poverty in one of the richest nations of the world. As concerned young people, you can play a part in helping our nation do a better job of living up to its democratic ideals.

REVIEW QUESTIONS

1. Was the War on Poverty successful?
2. What are some explanations advanced to account for the outcomes of the War on Poverty?
3. What is Herbert Gans' explanation for the continued existence of poverty?
4. How is unemployment related to poverty?
5. What might be an alternative goal to the elimination of poverty?
6. Does the existence of poverty contradict American ideals? If so, how?

SOURCE NOTES

Chapter 1

Our example of the young mother confronted with difficult choices was suggested by a remark of Dr. George Lamb, as quoted in the *Boston Globe Magazine* of December 15, 1985.

The income figures for states are taken from U.S. Department of Commerce statistics for 1986. The source for the contrasting counties in Alaska is Andrew Hacker, *U/S: A Statistical Portrait of the American People*, 1983.

The discussion of the measurement of poverty follows that of *Strategies Against Poverty in America*, by John Williamson et al.

The figures comparing poverty line income against national median income are drawn from Leonard Beeghley's *Living Poor in America*.

Chapter 2

Much of our historical discussion of poverty draws upon Walter Trattner's excellent *From Poor Law to Welfare State*.

The discussion of the New Deal era makes use of Frances Piven's and Richard Cloward's *Regulating the Poor*.

For descriptions of War on Poverty programs, we have drawn upon *Poverty and Public Policy*, by Michael Morris and John Williamson.

The account of the Family Assistance Plan of 1969 is largely drawn from Michael Harrington's *The New American Poverty*.

Chapter 3

The account of research on attitudes toward the poor follows John B. Williamson, "Beliefs About the Motivation of the Poor and Attitudes Toward Poverty Policy," *Social Problems* (June 1974).

William Ryan's remarks are taken from a *Boston Globe* article, "The Real Causes of Poverty" (February 15, 1987).

The discussion of poverty and dependency draws on an article by Michael Morris and John B. Williamson that is scheduled to appear in *Social Policy*. Titled "Workfare and the Poverty/Dependency Dilemma: The Inevitability of Trade-Off in Social Policy," it is slated for publication.

The San Diego County survey was described in an article by Michael Bernick, "How Welfare Can Work," in *Washington Monthly* (September 1985).

Brenner's "social costs" of unemployment were cited in *Corporate Flight*, by Barry Bluestone, Bennett Harrison, and Lawrence Baker (1981).

The Louv quotation is from his book *America II* (1985).

Sexton's figures on deindustrialization were cited in an article in *Dissent*, "The Epidemic of Homelessness," (Spring 1986).

Figures on unemployment and creation of new jobs from Bureau of Labor Statistics.

Chapter 4

The Martin Anderson quotation is from *Newsweek*, April 5, 1982.

Herbert Gans' article, "The Uses of Poverty: The Poor Pay All," appeared in *Social Policy*, July/August 1971.

The pastoral letter of the Catholic bishops is *Economic Justice for All: Catholic Social Teaching and the U.S. Economy*.

APPENDICES

THE AMERICAN CIVIC ANIMAL

In this section we will introduce some of the people who are actually involved with this issue. You will find out how you can get more information about the issue and how you can get involved yourself. You will also be introduced to a wise and friendly beast, a cool creature: The American Civic Animal. . . .

MIND:
An independent mind balances the facts and opinions heard by the ears with the feelings of the heart and soul and creates an independent opinion.

EARS:
Sensitive ears are able to hear the variety of opinions on every issue.

AGE:
Our scientists have recorded American Civic Animals active from the age of 7 to 107.

HABITAT:
The American Civic animal lives and participates in a variety of environments and climates ranging from voting booths to political conventions to study groups and soup kitchens.

HANDS:
Sometimes big and strong, other times detailed and soft, the hands put the independent opinions to work, turning beliefs into action.

EYES:
They range from deepest brown to brightest green to lightest blue, representing the magnificent diversity of American people.

MOUTH:
Big. The American Civic Animal likes to talk. However, for the mouth to make intelligent sounds, it needs to be accompanied by sensitive ears and an independent mind.

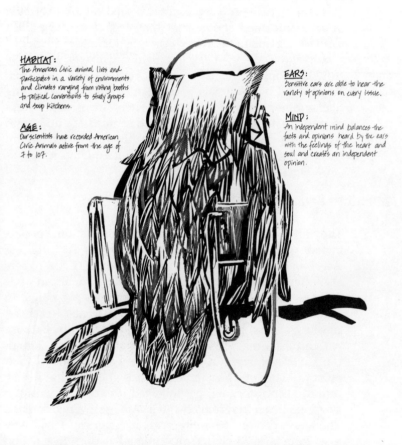

HABITAT:
The American Civic animal lives and Participates in a variety of environments and climates ranging from voting booths to political conventions to study groups and soup kitchens.

AGE:
Our scientists have recorded American Civic Animals active from the age of 7 to 107.

EARS:
Sensitive ears are able to hear the variety of opinions on every issue.

MIND:
An independent mind balances the facts and opinions heard by the ears with the feelings of the heart and soul and creates an independent opinion.

Activities:

Voting, reading, listening, organizing, demonstrating. It's quite difficult to narrow down just what American Civic Animals do. They are often spotted writing or calling their Congresspersons and representatives to keep these elected officials informed about what they feel. They have been sighted organizing summer activities for underprivileged youth and cooking meals for Senior Citizens who have trouble shopping for themselves. Perhaps you have seen American Civic Animals passing out leaflets at shopping malls or singing songs at rallies. There are as many ways to participate as there are issues that need attention and Americans eager to be involved. In the final examination, there is one trait that all American Civic Animals share:

American Civic Animals keep informed!

They often consume newspapers. Favorite national papers include the *New York Times*, the *Washington Post*, the *Los Angeles Times*, and *USA Today*, among others. Local papers also offer a wealth of regional information. American Civic Animals listen to television and radio news programs. In addition, they listen and talk with parents, teachers, coaches, sisters, brothers, neighbors, and friends. Because without listening, learning, and exchanging ideas, American Civic Animals can not wisely engage in one of their most fundamental and important activities: voting. If they cannot keep informed, get involved, or vote, they cannot stay free. In a letter from one great American Civic Animal, Thomas Jefferson, to another great American Civic Animal, John Adams, Jefferson summed it up: "If a nation expects to be ignorant and free . . . it expects what never was and never will be." The American Civic Animal realizes that one cannot be ignorant and free. The American Civic Animal gets involved first by keeping informed.

American Civic Animals are also joiners:

Observing the American Civic Animal 150 years ago, French author and traveller Alexis de Tocqueville said: "Americans of all ages, all stations of life, and all types of disposition are forever forming associations . . . of a thousand different types—religious, moral, serious, futile, very general and very limited, immensely large and very minute. . . . At the head of any new undertaking, where in France you would find the government or in England some territorial magnate, in the United States you are sure to find an association." The American Civic Animals of today are just as apt to join organizations and associations as they were in de Tocqueville's time.

American Civic Animals often work with national organizations, but they also like to quench their thirst for involvement in a number of community-oriented ways—such as neighborhood crime prevention groups, school support organizations, or environmental education programs.

The first step in becoming an American Civic Animal is to keep informed by reading a newspaper, reading a news magazine, or listening to the television or radio news programs. What if you want more information? What if you want to become even more involved? The following sections will give you some specific next steps and some specific organizations.

HOW TO START

- Find the correct organization or individual: if you are interested in addressing the issue of poverty in America, the Foreign Policy Association probably would not be the best organization for you to contact. Similarly, if you want to let your Senator know what you feel about a balanced Federal Budget, for example, you must know his/her name. The best place to find out the correct organization and/or name is in your local or school library. The Encyclopedia of Associations, which is usually in the reference section of a library, lists thousands of organizations and associations that deal with many different issues. Often the librarian can help you choose which one is appropriate for you. One easy way to find out the name of your Congressperson or Senator is to call the Capitol Switchboard in Washington, D.C., at (202) 224-3121. If no one you know can tell you the correct name, the operator who answers this number will.

- Find the correct address or telephone number. After you have found the appropriate organization or individual, you need to contact them. This can be done either in writing or by phone. (Remember: Calling is more expensive than writing!) If the organization is local, check your local phone book. If it is outside your area, check for the telephone number and address in the Encyclopedia of Associations. If you don't know the address or the telephone number, but you do know the town or city that the organization is in, call the area code for that city and then 555-1212. Tell the operator the city and the name of the organization and he/she will give you the correct telephone number. All members of Congress can be phoned by calling the Capitol Switchboard at the number listed in the paragraph above.

- Write or call. Many organizations and elected officials are pleased to hear from interested people. Many are eager to pass out information or to get help from energetic volunteers who care about the issues they deal with. Many organizations, including both political parties and citizens' action groups, welcome your participation. After keeping informed, getting involved is the next step to becoming an American Civic Animal.

- What happens then? If you're calling or writing for

information, ask for the specific type you are looking for. If you want to get involved with the organization, it's best if you tell them you would like to volunteer your services. Very few organizations can afford to pay their young employees, although some organizations do. Most organizations will allow flexible hours to allow for school or other employment. What you end up doing depends on the organization. You might be speaking with people on the phone; you might write letters; you might deliver meals or translate languages. While the work is not always thrilling, being involved in an issue you care about and seeing the difference you make can be very exciting. And that can be a lot of fun. The next section describes some organizations that deal with the specific issues addressed in this book.

RESOURCES

United Way

"The United Way works for all of us." But who works for the United Way? Football players like John Elway and Walter Payton volunteer their time. But what really makes the United Way effective are the millions of volunteers who donate their time and talents trying to make poverty disappear. In fact, in 1985, Americans contributed more than 16 billion hours—or more than 1,800,000 years of donated time. About 1,800,000 years ago, glaciers were still chasing dinosaurs off of North America. Indeed, over half of all Americans fourteen years old and older volunteer each year. Although these figures sound impressive, there is still much to be done, as you have learned. Although volunteers contributed an average of 3.5 hours per week, the average American spends about twice that amount of time daily in front of a television. Poverty is growing and the United Way needs your help.

Next to the federal government, United Way addresses the greatest variety of human care issues. Twenty-three hundred United Ways serve approximately thirty-seven thousand health and human care agencies, making it the largest volunteer network in the nation. One of the reasons the United Way is a tremendous organization to work with is that they offer so many different ways to volunteer. They will also help you find the volunteer project right for you. People work in programs ranging from alcoholism treatment to community health clinics to drug abuse treatment to job training to rape crisis relief to recreation to services for disabled individuals and shelter for the homeless.

United Way wants youth to get involved. A United Way

director said, "United Way is encouraging young people to get involved in community service because youth can help solve the social problems that our society faces." If you want to join in the fight against poverty, call the United Way listing in your phone book or write:

> United Way of America
> 701 North Fairfax Street
> Alexandria, Va. 22314-2045
> (703) 836-7100

ACTION

Four hundred thousand Americans fight poverty by volunteering through ACTION. If you want to get involved, ACTION is a great place to start. Built on the belief of neighbor helping neighbor, ACTION is the primary volunteer organization of the United States government. Whether the goal is to help adults learn to read, to help young people stay drug-free, to serve food to the hungry, or to provide companionship to the aged, ACTION programs and volunteers show that American citizens can join together to address the needs of a community and its people.

Donna M. Alvarado, the Director of ACTION, coordinates a number of different volunteer programs, including:

- **Student Service Learning Program:** If you are fourteen years old or older and want to get involved, this is the program for you. The SSLP encourages students to volunteer and serve in low-income communities. The program is especially valuable because it includes *training*. Experienced volunteers help the students develop job and service skills on site. Not only will you gain career experience, but you will also develop a sense of commitment to serve and help out in your community.
- **VISTA:** Volunteers In Service To America. VISTA volunteers work in urban areas, rural areas, or on Indian

reservations. They share their skills and experience in order to teach people how to read, build shelters, train workers for employment, and improve neighborhoods. In all fifty states, Puerto Rico and the Virgin Islands, VISTA volunteers are putting their hands to work trying to stop poverty.

- **Foster Grandparent Program:** The Foster Grandparent Program matches talented, experienced, and loving retired people with special youngsters who need guidance, companionship, and love. Both the young people and the retired folks benefit from helping and being needed.

If you are interested in any of these programs, or would like to learn more about how ACTION volunteers are making a difference right here in the United States, write:

ACTION
Washington, D.C. 20525

The Salvation Army

The estimated number of homeless persons in the United States has risen dramatically in recent years. The Salvation Army, an international Christian charitable movement founded in London in 1865, has dedicated itself to fighting the tragedy of the American homeless. The Salvation Army tries to give people a hot meal, a warm bed, and an opportunity to better their lives. In addition to offering three hundred beds a night, in 1985 the Atlanta division sponsored a jobs placement program which placed over seventeen hundred men and women in full-time jobs.

Helping the homeless is only one of the Salvation Army's many projects. With organizations in over eighty-five countries, the Army operates hospitals, counseling centers, rehabilitation programs, and employment services in all four corners of the globe. In the United States alone, the Salvation Army operates ten thousand centers with twenty-four thousand employees. If you are interested in getting involved in the Salvation Army, check your phone directory for the local chapter, or write:

> The Salvation Army
> 799 Bloomfield Avenue
> Verona, N.J. 07044

Save the Children

The longer a person or a family or a community is poor, the more likely they are to stay poor. Many poor grow dependent on outside help in order to survive. This dependence can erase confidence in their own ability to control their lives. Poverty lingers. One way to fight back against poverty is for people to get actively involved in improving their environment. This is the goal of Save the Children. In forty-five countries around the world, including the United States, Save the Children works with communities, helping people learn how to help themselves.

In the rural south, Save the Children is training women to run children's day care in their homes. This gives the women jobs, the children a warm, healthy place to play and learn, and the children's mothers the freedom to work or attend school. In New York City, children are learning how to grow food in school gardens. There are one hundred Save the Children field offices in American Indian communities stretching from California to Florida. In each of these communities, teams of Indian professionals and community volunteer committees work together fighting for education, health care, and job training. If you want to get involved with Save the Children's work in the United States and around the world write:

> Save the Children
> 54 Wilton Road
> Westport, Conn. 06880

Women's Equity Action League (WEAL)

The *feminization of poverty* is a popular phrase referring to the growing number of women who are forced into poverty. Some of these women are single parents trying to raise children. Some of these women are retirees trying to survive on Social Security. Many of these women have not had the educational and economic opportunities offered to men. WEAL, the Women's Equity Action League, is committed to helping these women. Working "behind the scenes" on legislative issues, WEAL supports the economic advancement of women. The issues on WEAL's agenda range from expanding equal opportunity laws, to fair coverage for women under social security, to affordable child-care services.

If you are interested in learning more about women's economic issues, WEAL is a terrific source. Their bimonthly newsletter covers the major pieces of Congressional legislation affecting women as well as other economic concerns in the courts and in the press. Write:

> Women's Equity Action League
> 1250 I Street, N.W.
> Washington, D.C. 20005

People United to Save Humanity (PUSH)

PUSH is a national organization dedicated to fighting poverty, unemployment, drugs, and political injustice. Founded in 1971 by Rev. Jesse Jackson and seventy national black leaders, PUSH grew out of Rev. Martin Luther King's and Jesse Jackson's "Operation Breadbasket," which was active in Chicago during the Civil Rights Movement. "Operation Breadbasket" organized economic boycotts and protests aimed at pressuring companies that sell to the black community to also support the black community with jobs.

PUSH is still active on the economic front. Corporations

such as General Foods, Burger King, Coca-Cola, and Seven-Up have negotiated covenants with PUSH pledging to employ black workers and be involved in black communities. PUSH also feeds hungry stomachs in Newark, Greensboro, Natchez, Cleveland, and Ethiopia. If you are interested in getting involved with PUSH's fight against poverty, call 312-FREEDOM, or write:

> PUSH
> P.O. Box 5432
> Chicago, Ill. 60680-9919

Youth Groups

Do you want to help fight poverty in your own community and learn how poverty affects people all around the world? Do other issues such as civil rights, nuclear war, hunger, and pollution interest you? Perhaps you should join a youth group in your community. Synagogues, churches, the Boy Scouts, and the Girl Scouts are just a few of the organizations sponsoring active youth groups in your neighborhood. Through these groups you can participate in a number of these important issues. Youth groups are also a great place to find friends and meet supportive adult sponsors who want you to get involved. Give them a try!

POVERTY AND HUNGER IN AMERICA

Hearing before the Subcommittee on Public Assistance and Un-employment Compensation of the Committee on Ways and Means, House of Representatives, Ninety-ninth Congress, April 30, 1985

STATEMENT OF J. LARRY BROWN, PH.D., MEMBER OF THE FACULTY, HARVARD SCHOOL OF PUBLIC HEALTH, AND CHAIRMAN, PHYSICIAN TASK FORCE ON HUNGER IN AMERICA

MR. BROWN. Two days ago, nationally syndicated cartoonist Garry Trudeau depicted Michael, in the "Doonesbury" strip, out looking for America's twenty million hungry citizens at the insistence of his minister.

Finally, in exasperation, Michael exclaimed, "But they're invisible." With a knowledgeable look on his face, his minister said in response, "See what I'm up against."

I appreciate the efforts of this subcommittee to look after the well-being of poor families and individuals in America. At no time in recent history has your challenge been so difficult.

Hunger and poverty, pain and suffering in this rich land generally are hidden from view and often are beyond the concerns of public officials. There is definitely another side to America—a side which I and other members of the Physician Task Force on Hunger in America found as we traveled across this land.

On the other side of America live millions of citizens in degradation and hopelessness. The plight limits our moral authority as a nation and undermines the benefits of a democratic society.

Benjamin Thompson lives on the other side of America.

This fifty-three-year-old army veteran lost his job when the Caterpillar plant closed in Peoria. His unemployment benefits ran out and his family now eats in a soup kitchen. With no electricity, his children do their studies by candle-light.

Of the Nation's 8.4 million jobless, 70 percent receive no unemployment benefits.

Randall Davis lives on the other side of America. Once a middle-class head of household, this Houston father of two was forced to desert his wife and children to make them eligible for AFDC so they could eat.

Twenty-seven states refuse to provide AFDC unless the father first leaves the home.

Timmy and Regina Johnson are four-year-old twins who live on the other side of America. Their mother's part time job, along with AFDC, fails to bring the family above the poverty line.

Over thirty-five million Americans live below poverty in the world's wealthiest nation.

I am invited to appear before you today because of my knowledge about hunger in America. But hunger is merely a symptom of poverty. It reflects the growing income disparity among people in our nation.

Nearly twenty years ago another group of physicians went into the backwaters of America. What they found was not pleasant:

> If you will go look, you will find America a shock-ing place. No other Western country permits such a large proportion of its people to endure the lives we press on the poor. To make four-fifths of a nation more affluent than any other people in history, we have degraded one-fifth mercilessly.

For a time our nation made great strides in improving this situation. The rate of poverty declined; the problem of hunger virtually vanished. But today we see clear deterioration. Of the thirty-five million Americans in poverty, an estimated twenty million go hungry every month.

Today I want to share what we learned about impoverishment from talking with the hungry and with those who try to feed them.

Impoverished Americans desperately want jobs. "If I could get another job," one unemployed mother told us, "I could feed my own family again. That's all I want." When our physicians went into homes to find empty refrigerators and children without milk, we asked what they most wanted. Almost without exception the answer was a job.

Hopefully, all will agree that these Americans should have jobs. But the central issue is what our nation is to do when the economy fails to employ our families. What do we do to protect them during their economic insecurity?

Compared to what our impoverished families need, the American safety net is really a band-aid. It is a hodge-podge of programs which is inadequate to raise families, and it penalizes those who try hard to get ahead. Let me provide several examples.

1. General Inadequacy of the Safety Net in America

The official poverty level represents the level below which our federal government determines it is impossible to meet minimal and decent living standards. In other words, the U.S. government recognizes that a family in poverty has not the minimal resources to meet the basic needs of its members.

It is in this light that we must face the fact that we force thirty-five million of our citizens to live below substandard levels.

Let us look briefly at the two basic programs for which an impoverished family may be eligible; the AFDC and food stamps. Today, in no state in the nation does the average family receiving benefits from these programs come even close to the poverty level.

In Alaska, the state with the highest benefits, a family of four receives only 89 percent of poverty when helped by these two programs. In Kansas, at the midpoint, that family gets 69 percent of poverty. And in Alabama, the state with the lowest assistance levels, parents are supposed to raise children on 46 percent of the poverty level.

In short, as a matter of public policy, America's treatment of its poorest families is indecent.

Under such circumstances, it is virtually impossible for most families to pull themselves out of difficult economic circumstances. By forcing families to live indecently, we foster disorganization and disintegration. Rather than providing a little extra to assist our people to get on their feet, we provide less. Our safety net programs are penny wise and pound foolish. In hurting our families, we hurt America.

2. Safety Net Programs Are More Punitive Than Helpful

When the government helps a middle-class youth attend college, or when it gives government aid to corporations, it is given in a positive manner. When aid is given to the poor, it is usually given in a punitive and mean-spirited manner.

As we traveled across the country, we found the "new poor" astounded at how they are treated now that they are penniless. As former taxpayers, they had assumed that government programs helped the downtrodden. Now that they are recipients, they enter a world of degradation and mean-spiritedness.

"To get help," one formerly middle-class woman told us in Raleigh, "we have to get rid of most of our accumulated resources, including our husbands."

In New Hampshire and New Mexico, we found families living in cars, rather than break apart to qualify for AFDC.

To require an American family to break apart to get help is meanness and punitiveness at its height. It destroys the family, by definition, and it serves to make America weaker as a result.

Another manifestation of safety net punitiveness is its no-net-gain nature. The programs, in concert, keep people in poverty. Fathers who get temporary work find their earnings deducted from their AFDC checks. Families which get a slight increase in AFDC find their food stamps decreased accordingly. Over and over families told us that "we just can't get ahead, no matter how hard we try." What the government adds to one pocket, it takes away from the other.

3. Conscious Government Policies Keep Poor Americans from Getting Help for Which They Are Eligible

You will remember that you and your colleagues last year passed legislation to prevent the administration from using administrative practices to cut eligible people from the Supplemental Security Disability Insurance Program. This commendable congressional action did not go far enough. Similar practices are being used to prevent eligible people from getting food stamps, AFDC, and other program assistance.

In the Food Stamp Program, for example, error rate sanctions against the states make it more likely that eligible applicants will be denied assistance. State officials tell us that federal requirements to reassess eligibility for many recipients place insurmountable obstacles before many needy people. And constant regulatory changes keep safety net programs in turmoil; computers have to be reprogrammed, regulations rewritten, workers retrained, and applicants reeducated.

As a consequence, needy and eligible applicants are prevented from getting the help they desperately need. The fact that poverty has gone up by six million people since 1980, but food stamp participation has gone down, is a reflection of these administrative practices.

We somehow hold to the fiction that we have a safety net which reflects the compassion of the American people. But the dramatic increase in poverty and the development of soup lines across our country stand as silent testimony to the fact that this is not true.

America has another side, and it is ugly.

Mr. Chairman, I must confess that in preparing to testify I found myself asking, "What's the use?" We know that hunger is an epidemic in America. We know that poverty is higher than at any point in the last twenty years. Reams and reams of expert testimony before committees of Congress provide ample documentation to prompt public officials to act.

Yet things get worse, not better. Hunger increases. More jobless go without unemployment benefits. More poor are without health care. Excess numbers of infants die as our infant mortality rate decline tails off.

Something is wrong in our nation that doctors and studies cannot fix.

Somehow our highest public officials are not adequately promoting life, liberty, and the pursuit of happiness. Our people suffer, and our leaders fail to respond.

Even as I speak, poor infants are being cut from the WIC Supplemental Feeding Program in a number of states— allegedly because America has not enough money to provide needed milk for them.

Yet we somehow have twenty-four billion dollars annually for tobacco subsidies. Why do we subsidize the deaths of 350,000 Americans from smoking, by denying the milk that will keep additional infants alive?

Two years ago I appeared before Senator Dole's Agriculture Subcommittee on Nutrition to report serious growth failures among poor children associated with hunger and malnutrition. I reported that unless we invested in nutrition programs, the likelihood was that I would be back the next year with further evidence of ill-health which inevitably occurs when nutrition is not adequate.

Mr. Chairman, that time has come, and my fear has come true.

I honestly do not want to return next year to have Congress ask me about our latest data. The question I have is whether our government cares. Do right-wingers not believe that our economic system is good enough to care for all our families? Do left-wingers care as much about programs of action as they do about criticizing their opponents? Does Congress care enough to exercise leadership to respond to pain and suffering?

This is the central question, and Congress needs no further expert testimony to answer. And I only hope that your colleagues in the Congress will follow your leadership in doing so.

Thank you very much.

CHILDREN IN POVERTY

Committee on Ways and Means, U.S. House of Representatives,
May 22, 1985

CHAPTER I. INTRODUCTION

In 1983, nearly fourteen million children, or more than one out of every five, lived below the official poverty line.[1] This was the highest poverty rate among children since the early 1960s. As of 1983, children comprised almost forty percent of the poor, and they and the adults living with them—twenty-four million people in all—made up more than two-thirds of the poverty population.

This paper examines patterns of childhood poverty and presents options intended either to reduce poverty among children or to alleviate its adverse effects. The remainder of this chapter discusses how poverty is measured, recent trends and current patterns of childhood poverty as officially measured, and the effects of using alternative definitions of poverty. Subsequent chapters examine issues that arise in dealing with childhood poverty, federal policies that currently address the poverty of children and

---

[1]Children are defined as all individuals under the age of eighteen. Congressional Budget Office tabulations of Census (Current Population Survey) data include in counts of children a small number of individuals under the age of eighteen who are not classified as children in certain Census tabulations. Accordingly, some published Census numbers may differ slightly from corresponding numbers appearing here. Moreover, in this paper, the words "families" and "households" generally mean families and households with children.

their families, and options for altering current federal efforts.[2]

The Incidence of Poverty Among Children

Which children, and how many, are poor depends on how poverty is measured. By the official Bureau of the Census yardstick, 22 percent of all children were poor in 1983, the highest poverty rate in two decades. Critics argue that official statistics misstate poverty, however, contending that poverty thresholds are set at the wrong levels and that families' incomes are not measured correctly. Nonetheless, across a wide range of alternative measures, poverty rates for children differ by only small amounts. Under none of the measures examined here does the magnitude of the problem shrink markedly.

Issues in Measuring Poverty

Measuring poverty entails establishing thresholds that specify the amount of resources assumed to be required to achieve a minimally adequate living standard, and comparing the resources available to each family with the appropriate threshold for that type of family. This raises two measurement issues:

- At what level should the thresholds be set?
- What resources should be counted in assessing whether a family falls below the appropriate threshold, and how should those resources be valued?

Any poverty threshold is necessarily arbitrary, reflecting the views of those who establish it regarding what consti-

---

[2]Considerably more detail on historical trends in poverty of children and on government programs is presented in a companion paper prepared by the Congressional Research Service and published elsewhere in this document. That paper also discusses factors associated with childhood poverty.

tutes a minimally adequate standard of living. One broad choice is whether to set absolute standards of minimum adequacy, or to fix thresholds relative to the economic position of the average citizen. With relative thresholds, the poverty line would float up or down with the standard of living in the broader population, while an absolute standard would fix the poverty line in real terms. Even absolute standards are defined in relation to the norms of the country involved, however. What is considered a minimally adequate standard of living in the United States, for example, would be viewed as very generous in many developing countries.

Deciding what resources should be considered in judging a family's well-being—and how those resources should be valued—involves choices about whether cash income should be measured before or after taxes are taken out, whether in-kind benefits such as health insurance or housing subsidies should be included, and whether assets should be taken into account. Most people contend that all resources that are available to meet immediate consumption needs, whether the resources are in cash or in kind, should be counted in judging whether a family is poor. Much less agreement exists, however, about what should be done with taxes, how in-kind benefits should be valued, and whether assets that do not provide current income—such as equity in homes—should be included in measuring a family's economic status.

The Official Measure and Trends in Childhood Poverty

The official poverty measure used in the United States was established two decades ago. It judges a family—and each member of the family—to be poor if the family has a cash income (counted before taxes are subtracted) that is less than thresholds originally set at three times the cost of a nutritionally adequate but minimum diet.[3] Although the specific poverty thresholds—which vary with family size and composition—are adjusted annually to take account of increases in the cost of living, neither the manner for setting thresholds nor the kinds of resources that are compared with those thresholds has been changed since the measure was first established.[4] In 1983, the official poverty threshold for a family of four was roughly $10,000. For other families, the thresholds varied from about $5,000 for a single person to just over $20,000 for families of nine or more people.

During the past twenty-five years, the official poverty rate among children first dropped sharply and then returned nearly to its previous levels (see Chart 1).[5] Several factors appear to be responsible for this pattern, including economic conditions, changes in household composition, and changes in federal policies. Although the poverty rate among children is likely to drop somewhat when data become available for 1984 and 1985, there is little indication that it will fall to the level of the late 1970s.

Between 1959 and 1969 the childhood poverty rate fell consistently, from approximately 26 percent to 14 percent. Furthermore, the number of poor children dropped by about 6.5 million, despite a 9 percent growth in the child population. Factors that may have contributed to this drop in poverty include: a generally strong economy, with declining unemployment and relatively low inflation; in-

---

[3]The factor of three was based on a 1955 survey of consumer expenditures that indicated that families of three or more spent an average of about one-third of their after-tax incomes on food.

[4]These two issues—setting thresholds and measuring resources—are the major areas of criticism of the official poverty definition. Further discussion of them and alternative measures are offered below.

[5]Much of this discussion of trends in poverty among children is drawn from Congressional Budget Office, "Poverty Among Children" (December 3, 1984). See this paper for a more in-depth analysis of the trends in childhood poverty.

creased real (that is, inflation-adjusted) government spending on poor children, particularly in the Aid to Families with Dependent Children (AFDC) program; and a relatively slow rate of increase in the proportion of children living in households headed by single women—a population that is especially likely to be poor.

The decline in the childhood poverty rate stopped in 1969. Over the course of the following decade the poverty rate among children rose slightly, though erratically, to roughly 16 percent in 1979. Even though the poverty rate fluctuated with economic cycles, its overall increase in this period appears to be primarily related to the increased proportion of children living in households headed by single women.

Between 1979 and 1983—the most recent years for which data are available—the child poverty rate rose sharply, from 16 percent to 22 percent, and the number of poor children rose by 3.7 million to 13.8 million (the highest number of poor children since the mid-1960s). This increase in poverty affected children in all household types, of all ages, and of all racial and ethnic groups. The growth in poverty rates appears to have been the result of the rapid inflation of 1979–1980, the severe back-to-back recessions of 1980 and 1981–1982, and the reductions in government spending on income-maintenance programs. The relatively small shifts in household composition that occurred during this brief period did not contribute significantly to the increase in the number of poor children.[6]

Although it is difficult to forecast poverty rates, it appears that the official child poverty rate is likely to decline

---

[6]Over the 1967–83 period, the portion of the poverty population comprising poor children plus adults in households with poor children grew from 65 percent to 70 percent. The increase in the poverty rate of these groups did not result in a correspondingly large increase in their share of the poverty population because of the offsetting decline in their share of the total population.

as data covering the current economic expansion become available. While the extent of any further decline is unknown, several factors suggest that it is unlikely that the poverty rate will return to its pre-recession (1979) level. First, if the unemployment rate follows the pattern assumed in the most recent Congressional Budget Office (CBO) economic assumptions, it will remain above its 1979 level and thus impede a drop in childhood poverty. Second, the growing proportion of children who live in households headed by single women is continuing to contribute to a slight upward drift in the poverty rate that is largely independent of cyclical changes in the economy. Finally, future federal budgetary constraints make large increases in income-security benefits (which would reduce poverty) unlikely over the next several years. On the other hand, if the recovery is sufficiently strong and sustained, it could offset these factors. Nonetheless, poverty is almost certain to continue to be common among children and the adults who take care of them.

Characteristics of Poor Children

Although poverty is found among all groups of children, the poverty rate varies somewhat with the age of the child, and varies greatly with household composition, ethnicity and race, and whether the children are living in inner cities, suburbs, or rural areas.[7] In 1983, one out of four preschool children was poor—slightly more than the one-fifth of all school-age children who are living in poverty.

Poverty is much more common among children in households headed by single women than among two-

---

[7]Data in this section are from Department of Commerce, Bureau of the Census, "Characteristics of the Population Below the Poverty Level: 1983," Current Population Reports, Consumer Income Series P-60, No. 147 (February 1985), pp. 31–38 and 40–42.

parent households.[8] In 1983, 55 percent of the children living in households headed by single women were poor—more than four times the rate for children in two-parent households. Children from households headed by single women constitute almost 20 percent of the entire population of children, but they make up almost half of all poor children.

Minority children are much more likely to be poor than are nonminority children, although substantial numbers of the latter group are also poor. In 1983, 47 percent of all black children and 38 percent of all Hispanic children were poor, compared with 15 percent of all nonminority children.[9] Minority children comprise one-fourth of the entire child population, but they make up almost half of all poor children. Poverty rates are highest among minority children in households headed by single women. In 1983, about seven out of every ten minority children in households headed by single women were poor.

Finally, poverty is more common among children who live either in central portions of metropolitan areas or in nonmetropolitan areas. In 1983, 31 percent of all children living in central cities of metropolitan areas and 24 percent of children living in nonmetropolitan areas were poor,

---

[8]In this discussion, families with two parents and families where the father is the single parent are combined into the "two-parent" category, because data about households headed by single men are available for only a small sample. Although the poverty rate of these households is higher than that of two-parent households, it is lower than that of households headed by single women.

[9]Census publications define as "Spanish Origin" all who classify themselves as such, regardless of race. Thus, the Census racial and ethnic categories overlap; Spanish Origin individuals are tabulated both as such and as either white or black. In this discussion, all persons in the Spanish Origin category are classified as Hispanic and are not counted as either black or "nonminority." The "nonminority" category is constructed by substracting all Hispanics from the count of whites and thus is nearly equivalent to "non-Hispanic white," since almost all Hispanics are classified as white.

compared with 13 percent of children living in noncentral (primarily suburban) portions of metropolitan areas. More than three-fourths of all poor children live either in central cities or in nonmetropolitan areas (39 percent and 37 percent, respectively); the remaining poor children live in noncentral portions of metropolitan areas.

PROMOTING THE WELFARE
OF AMERICANS IN THE 1980s

*President's Commission for a National Agenda for the Eighties,
Report of the Panel on Government and the Advancement of
Social Justice, Health, Welfare, Education and Civil Rights*

The present public welfare system consists of layer upon
layer of outdated, sometimes redundant programs. The
bureaucratic complexity of the system helps to defeat its
object: Many persons in need do not receive adequate
assistance.

Some of the needs overlooked by the public systems are
supplied by private charities and other nonprofit organizations, whose contributions are, and will continue to be,
vital to the public good. Nevertheless, the design and
implementation of public welfare programs clearly require
significant improvement. The Panel is of the opinion that
this can best be accomplished by replacing the current
maze of programs with a minimum security income.

It cannot be denied that the multiplicity of programs in
place today embodies an approach that has not been entirely successful. Poverty persists in America—official estimates placed the number of the poor at twenty-five million
in 1976. This figure comes from Bureau of the Census
estimates of how many people have incomes below the
official poverty standard. The standard is derived by com-
puting the cost of a "temporary, low budget, nutritious
diet" and multiplying that result by a constant chosen to
represent the amount of income a family should spend on
food. The official poverty standard is modest; in 1978 the
poverty level for a typical urban family of four was $6,665.[1]

Some experts dispute the official statistics because the

value of such programs as food stamps and Medicaid is not included. By the most optimistic estimates, ones with which this Panel has serious disagreements, eight million Americans remain poor.

The poor suffer real hardship. Often they do not get enough to eat, and they experience more than their share of sickness. Those poor families that manage to obtain welfare face a harsh existence. An Illinois family on welfare, for example, receives about $500 a month. If $215 is spent for shelter and $149 is used to purchase food, only $136 remains to cover the cost of clothing, household supplies, and everything else. Those who fail to obtain welfare live even more debilitating lives.[2]

Poverty and Social Expenditures

The American poor are not randomly distributed. Women account for about two-thirds of the adult poor, and nonwhites are more than twice as likely to be poor as are whites. In fact, almost 16 percent of all nonwhite families were poor in 1976. Government programs do aid nonwhites; but they actually benefit whites more than nonwhites.[3]

The incidence of poverty also varies by region. Recent data show that the South has twice as many poor people as do the North Central states, even after welfare and Social Security benefits are paid.[4]

More disturbing than this persistence of poverty along sexual, racial, and regional lines are recent trends in income levels. Between 1968 and 1972 real income per household rose only 1.7 percent, and the number of families placed in poverty began to increase. Between 1972 and 1976, this trend was exacerbated; real income per household actually dropped 5.0 percent.[5]

It has been argued that the eradication of poverty is an unreasonable goal, one that does not belong on an agenda for the 1980s. The poorest of poor Americans, after all, lives well by world standards. In addition, some analysts think that the nation already spends too much on social welfare, and that the creation of a large welfare establishment has unintentionally erected barriers that prevent people from rising above poverty. The nation, in this view, may have reached the limit of its ability to do good.

The United States does spend a great deal of money for social purposes. Between 1960 and 1975, social welfare expenditures more than quadrupled to $1,319 dollars per capita.* Expenditures that fall more strictly under the heading of welfare have increased at an even greater rate, rising from $34 per capita in 1950 to approximately $187 in 1975. Some $394 billion, a figure equivalent to 19.3 percent of the gross national product (GNP), were spent on social welfare in 1978. In 1965 ths share was 11.5 percent.

Social welfare expenditures reached a peak of 20.4 percent of the gross national product in 1975. Their share of the gross national product and of total government spending has declined since 1976. The real rate of growth in social welfare expenditures declined to 2.5 percent by 1979.[6] Because of inflation and other factors that constrain the federal budget, this decline in the growth of social welfare expenditures will probably continue; only a severe recession will arrest the trend.

The Institutional Setting

The only rationale for the existing welfare system is historical. Each program represents a small piece of history, embodying a politically acceptable approach to a particular problem at the time of the program's creation. There are at least five distinct types of welfare programs, each of which reflects a different approach to aiding the poor or ending

---

*The term "social welfare" as used here includes social insurance, public aid, health and medical programs, veterans' programs, education, and housing. Figures are given in current dollars.

poverty. Briefly described, the five types of programs are designed to:

- Aid members of the "deserving poor";
- Define minimum standards;
- Insure against loss of income;
- Support the purchase of essentials; and
- Provide, or promote, opportunity

Today's system is an uncoordinated collection of past efforts to accomplish not one end, but many.

Aid to the "Deserving Poor"

In the oldest kind of program, the government aids those members of the community who are unable to care for themselves: the very young, the very old, and the disabled. The traditional means of helping such dependent persons was to place them under the care of a family or of the community itself.

In time, institutions such as orphanages and poor farms began to replace this informal system. By 1900, states permitted counties to provide cash grants to the deserving poor. Reliance on local governments to provide aid to the poor ended with the passage of the Social Security Act in 1935, when Congress authorized federal aid to the states for grants to the needy elderly, the blind, and dependent children.

The creation of these federal public assistance categories marked the beginning of what is now called welfare. The basic approach was inherited from the earlier state laws. If a person could show that he was elderly, blind, or a dependent child, and if he could demonstrate need, then he received a cash payment from the local authorities. The federal government paid a portion of the local government's expenses.

With the entry of the federal government into the field of welfare, the informality and fexibility characteristic of local arrangements gave way to rigid categories mandated at the federal level. This approach offered the benefit of what experts call target efficiency—it reached only the poor—but it left gaps in coverage. One had to be more than poor to receive government aid; one had to belong to the "deserving poor," to be old, young, blind, or permanently and totally disabled.

Definition of Minimum Standards

Another type of welfare program, one that defined minimum standards, began during the Progressive Era at the turn of the century. Progressive reformers advocated, and saw passed, protective labor legislation that set minimum standards for working conditions. Typical laws of this kind included child labor laws, maximum hours and minimum wage requirements, safety standards, and workers' compensation laws.

These laws answered perceived needs of the Progressive Era. It should be recalled that women were discouraged from working in those years, and that many Americans were concerned about the disruptions caused by rapid immigration. Conditions differ today. No longer does the nation wish to exclude women or those of foreign origin from the labor force. No longer is there a strict distinction between occupational and nonoccupational problems; no longer does the government limit itself to promulgating social welfare standards, instead taking an active role in maintaining incomes and in protecting people against the risk of sickness. Despite these circumstantial changes, the turn-of-the-century program of minimum standards endures as an American approach to social welfare.

This "standards of decency" approach is beneficial in some respects; however, it has the drawback of sometimes substituting the wish for the deed, particularly in the case of minimum wages. Mandating minimum wages does not ensure that everyone will receive them; it may mean instead that employers choose not to hire those workers whose productivity fails to merit the minimum wage. Ironically, it is the young, the disabled, and the members of minority groups—precisely those whom society seeks to protect through minimum wage legislation—who may suffer by that wage's existence.*

Social Insurance

A third type of welfare program, government insurance against loss of income, owes its origin to the passage of the Social Security Act in 1935. The Act created an old-age insurance program; its reach has since been broadened to include survivors' insurance (1939), disability insurance (1956), and health insurance for the elderly (1965). As a result, a program that cost $23.5 million in 1940 now costs $9 billion (in current dollars) and reaches 3.5 million people each month.

Unemployment compensation, or temporary payments to workers laid off from their jobs, also began in 1935 with the passage of the Social Security Act. This program differed from Social Security in that it was run by the states instead of the federal government. Such program details as which workers were eligible for benefits and the number of weeks they could receive benefits varied greatly from state to state. From a national perspective, the unemployment compensation program, like Social Security, has expanded greatly; the program cost $500 million in 1939 and $17 billion in 1975 (in current dollars).[7]

President Roosevelt, in describing Social Security and unemployment compensation, and federal officials, in administering the programs, took pains not to connect the words "welfare" and "social insurance." Social Security was portrayed as a reliable government insurance program

---

*Among the measures being discussed currently is a differential in the minimum wage applied to youth.

to which all Americans paid premiums and from which all Americans received benefits. These benefits came to people as a matter of right, and the program provided money to rich and poor alike. Programs for the poor, officials believed, made poor programs.

Both Social Security and unemployment insurance, however, contained what could be seen as welfare elements. To deal with the problem of paying everyone adequate benefits, for instance, planners allowed low-wage earners a higher rate of return on their Social Security and unemployment compensation premiums than high-wage earners.

Social Security possessed the additional feature of taking money from workers and giving it to the elderly and disabled. Under the original design of the program, a worker and his employer deposited money in a Social Security account; the worker was to receive it back with interest upon his retirement. In an effort to broaden coverage, raise benefits, and lower payroll taxes, Congress altered the system so that it could be run on a pay-as-you-go basis. After 1939, current workers and their employers paid for the current group of retirees and disabled workers.

The insurance analogy helped to establish Social Security and enabled the program to grow. The very size and success of the program, in turn, produced demands that it do more than insure against loss of income, that it help to deal with some of America's welfare problems. As a public assistance vehicle, however, Social Security was flawed. First, the program failed to reach people outside the labor force who had no income to insure. Second, it developed funding problems that were related to its special feature of relying upon employer and employee contributions. Benefit levels were increased faster than were payroll taxes; this led to occasional shortages in the fund that was used to pay the benefits. (When the postwar generation retires after 2010, this problem will become severe.) Finally, a program built upon the social assumptions of the 1930s contained many outdated elements by the 1980s. Divorced women, for example, received less than did married women.

Aid to Purchase Essentials

The intent of a fourth type of government program is to ensure that participants are able to purchase certain essential goods and services, such as food or medical care. Food stamps, for example, may in their modern form be traced to an unsuccessful New Deal experiment and a Kennedy Administration program of 1961.

The food stamp program was extended to the entire nation by Congress in 1964, but it experienced only modest growth until late in the decade.[8] The food stamp program expanded rapidly between 1968 and 1971 for two reasons. First, themes sounded by the Robert Kennedy campaign and by civil rights activists and other reformers made the existence of hunger in an otherwise affluent society unacceptable. Something had to be done to feed the poor quickly, and the food stamp program was conveniently at hand, ready for increased appropriations. Second, members of the Nixon Administration and others who favored simplifying the welfare system saw in food stamps an approach that provided the poor with essentials and could be—in fact, was—administered at the local level. Conservative and liberal members of Congress, able to agree on little else, compromised on the expansion of food stamps. In a series of amendments, benefit levels were increased, uniform eligibility standards were promulgated, and all counties were required to have a program. One authority has called the expansion of food stamps "the most important change in public welfare policy since the passage of the Social Security Act in 1935."[9] The growth of Medicaid, a program that enabled the poor to purchase medical care, matched that of food stamps.

These programs fill real needs and help to remedy gaps

in the American welfare system. Still, these essential purchase programs raise the question of whether the government knows better than the individual what it is good for him to have. Essential purchase aid, in short, owes more to political expediency than to rational planning.

Promotion of Opportunity

The four classes of welfare programs already discussed involve maintaining the needy. A fifth kind of government aid attempts to raise the poor above poverty by education, rehabilitation, provision of a special social service, or placement in a job.

Welfare programs featuring such government sponsorship of expanded opportunity originated in the 1920s when the benefits of rehabilitation were recognized. Instead of allowing a person to become a welfare recipient, he could be trained, counseled, or cured to become a productive citizen. This transformation was doubly attractive, for it contributed to the public as well as the individual good. Among the programs that followed this approach were vocational education and vocational rehabilitation.

These efforts were not meant to include large numbers of people. Each program worked selectively, concentrating on a few clients, and all were run by the casework principle. Vocational rehabilitation, for example, was a painstaking process of direct interviews between a disabled client and a counselor. Each counselor could handle only 75 to 100 cases at any one time; coupled with the small number of counselors, this constraint severely limited the number of people the program could serve. As the counselors were forced to choose among clients, they often selected the most promising clients, those who needed the least help. Rehabilitation programs, therefore, served the mildly impaired and not the severely disabled.

Government efforts to improve opportunity suffered from the fact that they were only as strong as the economy.

Almost all of the programs took as their object the eventual placement of their clients into the general labor market. In times of high employment, such as the 1920s, the approach worked relatively well; in hard times the approach almost always failed. These programs, then, failed to deal with the distress caused by recession or depression.

After World War II, an increase in the welfare rolls and an emerging belief that the nation had the means to end poverty prompted a new interest in government promotion of opportunity. The problems of the older programs were forgotten as the nation launched a new series of programs. In 1962, a well-known congressional supporter spoke of a "realistic program which will pay dividends on every dollar invested. It can move some persons off the assistance rolls entirely, enable others to attain a high degree of self-confidence and independence, encourage children to grow strong in mind and body."[10] Two years later, President Johnson announced the start of the War on Poverty by observing, "We are not content to accept the endless growth of relief rolls or welfare rolls. We want to offer the forgotten fifth of our people opportunity and not doles."[11]

Although the optimism engendered by this hopeful rhetoric faded, a large social service establishment remained. In addition to the programs begun in the 1920s, many states offered a full range of supplementary services, often including day care, family planning, and special transportation programs. In fiscal year 1979, in fact, federal spending for social services amounted to nearly $2.6 billion.[12]

Despite its shortcomings, government promotion of opportunity continues to be a politically attractive means of aiding the poor. Conservative politicians have supported it as an alternative to public assistance, one that is expected to reduce government spending in the long run. Liberal politicians have regarded the strategy as one way of increasing vital social services. Members of both groups like the implicit idea of a permanent solution, through jobs, to the welfare problem.

The most recent example of this type of welfare program is the Comprehensive Employment and Training Act (CETA) of 1974.* This consolidation of federal manpower programs includes social services for adults who are the victims of structural unemployment. In addition, CETA authorizes the Secretary of Labor to provide special services to such groups as native Americans, migrant and seasonal farm workers, displaced homemakers, the handicapped, persons of limited English-speaking ability, offenders, older workers, and public assistance recipients. Half-buried under layers of confusing regulations and dense jargon, government promotion of opportunity remains an important type of U.S. welfare program.

Inherited Programs

There are, then, not one but at least five types of government welfare programs. The nation also maintains a large number of private charities, and from an individual's point of view, the result is often confusion. For example, a recently widowed mother of several children, one of whom is disabled, may now apply to seven federal programs for aid. In a typical jurisdiction, she will have to go to at least four different offices, fill out at least five different forms, and answer some 300 separate questions. The programs may treat the information obtained from these forms differently; the value of the same care, for example, is almost sure to differ from program to program. Fourteen hundred pieces of information may be needed just to determine accurately the level of the woman's income. This illustration underscores the 1974 finding of a congressional subcommittee:

*The CETA program is discussed in more detail in the report of the Economics Panel.

Instead of forming a coordinated network . . . our . . . income maintenance programs are an assortment of fragmented efforts that distribute income to various persons for various purposes, sometimes on conflicting terms and with unforeseen results.[13]

Despite pleas for simplification, the separate tactics of government aid to the "deserving poor," definition of minimum standards, insurance against loss of income, aid to purchase essentials, and promotion of opportunity all contribute to the present American welfare system. This system is, in effect, a catalogue of historical approaches to social welfare; it features the very oldest as well as the very newest ideas. Attempts to reform the current set of welfare programs must relieve the confusion caused by the persistence of programs long after the time of their enactment.

Notes

1. U.S. Department of Commerce, Bureau of the Census, *Current Population Reports,* series P-60, no. 115 (Washington, D.C., 1978), p. 15.
2. President's Commission for a National Agenda for the Eighties, Hearings in Chicago, Ill., July 22, 1980, transcript. Testimony of the Public Welfare Coalition for a Humane Public Aid Program in Illinois.
3. Diane Pearce, "The Feminization of Poverty: Women, Work, and Welfare," *Urban and Social Review* 11:28–36; U.S. Commission on Civil Rights, *Social Indicators of Equality for Minorities and Women* (Washington, D.C., 1978), pp. 47–67; Congressional Budget Office, *Poverty Status of Families Under Alternative Definitions of Income,* Background Paper 19 (Washington, D.C., 1977).
4. *Poverty Status,* p. 16.
5. Sheldon Danziger and Robert Plotnick, "Has the War on Poverty Been Won?" Paper delivered at the Second Annual Middlebury College Conference on Economic Issues, Middlebury, Vt., April 1980.
6. U.S. Department of Health and Human Services, Social Security Administration, Office of Research and Statistics, "Social Welfare Expenditures, Fiscal Year 1978," research and statistics note (Washinton, D.C., 1980).
7. Daniel S. Hamermesh, *Jobless Pay and the Economy* (Baltimore, Md., 1977); U.S. Department of Health, Education, and Welfare, Social

Security Administration, Office of Research and Statistics, "Monthly Benefit Statistics" (Washington, D.C., 1979).

8. Maurice McDonald, *Food Stamps and Income Maintenance* (New York, 1973).

9. President's Commission, Hearings, testimony of Richard Nathan.

10. Senator Ribicoff, as quoted in Gilbert Steiner, *Social Insecurity: The Politics of Welfare* (Chicago, 1966), p. 39. The Senator is referring to the Public Welfare Amendments of 1962.

11. Lyndon B. Johnson, "Remarks upon Signing the Economic Opportunity Act, August 20, 1964," *Public Papers of the Presidents 1963–64* (Washington, D.C., 1965), 2:988.

12. U.S. Congress, General Accounting Office, "U.S. Income Security System Needs Leadership, Policy, and Effective Management" (Washington, D.C., 1980), p. 22.

13. U.S. Congress, Joint Economic Committee, Subcommittee on Fiscal Policy, "Income Security for Americans: Recommendations of the Public Welfare Study" (Washington, D.C., 1974).

CHILDREN IN POVERTY

*Hearing before the Subcommittee on Public Assistance and Un-
employment Compensation of the Committee on Ways and
Means, House of Representatives, Ninety-Ninth Congress, May
22, 1985*

STATEMENT OF VELMA W. BURKE, SPECIALIST IN SOCIAL LEGISLATION, AND HEAD OF THE INCOME MAINTENANCE SECTION, EDUCATION AND PUBLIC WELFARE DIVISION, CONGRESSIONAL RESEARCH SERVICE, LIBRARY OF CONGRESS, ACCOMPANIED BY JEAN GRIFFITH AND RICHARD RIMKUNAS

MRS. BURKE. Child poverty is a persistent problem, and for many years it has been growing, as the chairman said. In the ten years from 1973 to 1983, it grew more than 50 percent. An extra eight children per 100 were added to the poverty population in that decade.

This lifted the child poverty rate to 22.2 children per 100. That is the highest level since the mid-1960s. The increase in the rate of poverty of children was so great in this decade that although the total population of children in the country declined by six million, we had an extra four million poor children. Our study explores the growth and the persistence of child poverty. It deals only with income poverty. It does not deal with other impoverishments, sometimes cited by economists, such as education poverty, health poverty, transportation poverty. We deal only with income poverty. We did not examine the possible impacts of insufficient money upon a child's health, his education, his aspirations, his work ethic.

The method that we used to examine this problem was to study and to examine income data from the Census

Bureau relating to children for a number of years, from 1968 to 1983. Thanks to modern technology, our industrious team efforts, and computers, we analyzed data on 2.5 million persons. The file that we amassed provides more information about the economic status of children than had been put together before. How did we use this data? We analyzed the poverty status of children in ways that supplement what the Census Bureau normally does.

As you probably know, when the Census Bureau decides who is poor, it looks at the cash income of the family before paying taxes, and it compares the cash income of the family to a yardstick, the poverty threshold. That threshold is roughly the sum of money equal to three times the cost of the thrifty food plan. The threshold is adjusted for family size, and to some extent for family composition.

We used that yardstick and applied it at different stages of the economic life of the family. We first used the yardstick to calculate how many children were poor on the basis of their market income only; how many children were poor if you looked just at the family earnings and other market income. We called that the market income poverty rate. We looked at trends in that rate.

Now, the government can intervene, to assist children who are poor with cash payments of two kinds: first, social insurance, and second, welfare, which is adjusted for need. So we looked at the contribution of each category. We calculated the poverty rates after social insurance and before welfare, and then we calculated the poverty rates after all cash payments. The last calculation would be equivalent to what the Census Bureau does; it gives us the official poverty rate. It happens that federal outlays for noncash aid to needy persons now far exceed those made in the form of cash. So we also did some calculations to see how trends are affected and poverty rates are affected if you count noncash benefits; and Senator Moynihan's comparison of the poverty rate of children and the aged makes use of that kind of data. If you take into account major noncash benefits, including medical benefits, then indeed the aged have a poverty rate that is about one-sixth that of children.

Our report is organized around, I would say, five major questions, and the briefing will follow the same order.

First, the extent of the problem; second, the extent to which poverty rates are influenced by household composition; third, the extent to which poverty rates reflect earnings of different kinds of families; fourth, the capacity of economic growth to influence poverty rates; and finally, the effect of government transfers upon poverty rates.

Chart 1, which is in your packet and also up on the easel, displays the incidence of poverty for three age groups from 1966 to 1983, and it is immediately apparent that in 1974 children displaced the aged as the poorest age group.

MRS. BURKE. The rise from 1973 to 1983, as we said, is more than 50 percent, and the end result in 1983 was that 22.2 children per 100 were poor. Now, that rate is about 50 percent above the rate for the aged, so if you measure the comparison in cash you get a 50 percent higher rate for the aged. The population of poor children changed somewhat over this period. Back in 1966, 59 percent of the children were white. In 1983, the share rose to 63 percent because in this period the population of poor children became somewhat more white. Much of that occurred in the last few years. The red line, showing child poverty incidence, ascends especially fast from 1978 to 1983. That was a time, as we will be discussing, when poverty rates rose sharply for children in two-parent families.

People often ask why poverty rates for the aged went down so very rapidly, and I would say that the short answer is that we have made a commitment to the economic security of the aged, which is illustrated in a couple of ways. The Social Security Program covered most of the aged in the period shown. Also, in the early 1970s the program received a high ad hoc benefit increase, and then in 1975 had its first automatic cost of living adjustment.

In addition, in 1974 we inaugurated a guarantee of cash income for needy aged persons, the Supplemental Security Income Program, and that program also has benefits which are adjusted for inflation.

In the case of children, we do not have a counterpart program. The Social Security Act includes a program for needy children called AFDC [Aid to Families with Dependent Children], but its benefits are set by states and have been eroded by inflation, as you will see.

There also are Social Security "insurance" benefits for children. For children to receive Social Security, they do not have to pass a test of need. Instead, they have to have lost a parent through death, or they have to have a parent who has retired or is disabled, and we will see later that the federal dollars spent for children and their parent caretakers in the Social Security Program exceed the federal dollars spent on the AFDC Program. So social insurance for children is also important.

The poverty income gap of children has increased. We have not only had a rise in the incidence of poverty among children, there also has been a rise in their poverty income gap, which is the shortfall, the amount of cash by which a family's income is short of its poverty threshold. The aggregate income shortfall for children increased from $10 billion in 1973 to $15.9 billion in 1983 in constant dollars.

Who were the 13.8 million poor children in 1983? Well, that is summarized on the first page. I will not go into great detail, but I will call your attention to the fact that they are roughly divided between children in female-headed families and children in male-present families, the latter being two-parent families and those in which the father is raising children alone. Almost one-third of the poor children had separated or divorced mothers, and one-eighth of the poor children, 1.8 million, had never-married mothers.

Table 1, which is on page 5, gives a picture of the variety of rates, and I guess it suffices to say that a child's chances of being poor are varied, depending upon race, family type, and presence of the father in the home.

MRS. BURKE. In general, a black child was almost three times as likely to be poor as a white. Almost one-half of the black children were poor, more than one-third of the Hispanics, and about one-sixth of the whites.

Family type has a profound influence upon poverty. In a female-headed family a black child has a chance of more than two-thirds of being poor. The group with the highest probability of poverty is children of never-married mothers. Overall, three out of four such children were poor in 1983, and regardless of race; the poverty rate exceeded 70 percent for whites, for blacks, or Hispanics.

You will note that two-parent families show a variation in poverty rates as well. The rate for male-present families in the black community was double the poverty rate for whites; and in the case of Hispanics, it was more than double.

Table 1: Poverty Rates per 100 Children by Family Type and Race, 1983[1]

Children	White	Black	Hispanic	All children under 18 years
Total	17.3	46.7	38.2	22.2
In female-headed families (total)	47.6	68.5	70.5	55.8
Mothers: Never married	71.3	77.2	85.8	75.1
Separated or divorced	47.3	66.8	70.1	53.5
Widowed	27.9	60.7	38.9	41.1
In male-present families	11.9	23.8	27.3	13.5

[1]These rates refer to all children under age 18 and differ from those for related children, which are used in this report for trend data.

I should mention that there are distinctions between groups of poor people other than their incidence of poverty. As Mr. Campbell has pointed out, there is a distinction between those who are long-term poor and those who are short-term poor, and we find in general that two-thirds of the children who are poor at any time during their childhood—we define that as a fifteen-year period—are poor for no more than four years, but about one-seventh of those who are poor at one time in their childhood are poor for at least ten years. Those who are persistently poor are demographically somewhat different from those who are short-term poor: Over 90 percent of these children are black, and they tend to live in the South, in rural areas, and to not have a father at home.

The War on Poverty

The material that follows is taken from Lyndon Johnson's 1964 State of the Union Address, in which he announced the War on Poverty.

Annual Message to the Congress on the State of the Union. January 8, 1964

Mr. Speaker, Mr. President, Members of the House and Senate, my fellow Americans:

I will be brief, for our time is necessarily short and our agenda is already long.

Last year's congressional session was the longest in peacetime history. With that foundation, let us work together to make this year's session the best in the nation's history.

Let this session of Congress be known as the session which did more for civil rights than the last hundred sessions combined; as the session which enacted the most far-reaching tax cut of our time; as the session which declared all-out war on human poverty and unemployment in these United States; as the session which finally recognized the health needs of all our older citizens; as the session which reformed our tangled transportation and transit policies; as the session which achieved the most effective, efficient foreign aid program ever; and as the session which helped to build more homes, more schools, more libraries, and more hospitals than any single session of Congress in the history of our republic.

All this and more can be done. It can be done by this summer, and it can be done without any increase in spending. In fact, under the budget that I shall shortly submit, it can be done with an actual reduction in federal expenditures and federal employment.

Unfortunately, many Americans live on the outskirts of hope—some because of their poverty, and some because of their color, and all too many because of both. Our task is to help replace their despair with opportunity.

This administration today, here and now, declares unconditional war on poverty in America. I urge this Congress and all Americans to join with me in that effort.

It will not be a short or easy struggle, no single weapon or strategy will suffice, but we shall not rest until that war is won. The richest nation on earth can afford to win it. We cannot afford to lose it. One thousand dollars invested in salvaging an unemployable youth today can return forty thousand dollars or more in his lifetime.

Poverty is a national problem, requiring improved national organization and support. But this attack, to be effective, must also be organized at the state and local level and must be supported and directed by state and local efforts.

For the war against poverty will not be won here in Washington. It must be won in the field, in every private home, in every public office, from the courthouse to the White House.

The program I shall propose will emphasize this cooperative approach to help that one-fifth of all American families with incomes too small to even meet their basic needs.

Our chief weapons in a more pinpointed attack will be better schools, and better health, and better homes, and better training, and better job opportunities to help more Americans, especially young Americans, escape from squalor and misery and unemployment rolls where other citizens help to carry them.

Very often a lack of jobs and money is not the cause of poverty, but the symptom. The cause may lie deeper—in our failure to give our fellow citizens a fair chance to develop their own capacities, in a lack of education and training, in a lack of medical care and housing, in a lack of decent communities in which to live and bring up their children.

But whatever the cause, our joint federal-local effort must pursue poverty, pursue it wherever it exists—in city slums and small towns, in sharecropper shacks or in migrant worker camps, on Indian reservations, among whites as well as Negroes, among the young as well as the aged, in the boom towns and in the depressed areas.

Our aim is not only to relieve the symptom of poverty, but to cure it and, above all, to prevent it. No single piece of legislation, however, is going to suffice.

We will launch a special effort in the chronically distressed areas of Appalachia.

We must expand our small but our successful area redevelopment program.

We must enact youth employment legislation to put jobless, aimless, hopeless youngsters to work on useful projects.

We must distribute more food to the needy through a broader food stamp program.

We must create a National Service Corps to help the economically handicapped of our own country as the Peace Corps now helps those abroad.

We must modernize our unemployment insurance and establish a high-level commission on automation. If we have the brain power to invent these machines, we have the brain power to make certain that they are a boon and not a bane to humanity.

We must extend the coverage of our minimum wage laws to more than two million workers now lacking this basic protection of purchasing power.

We must, by including special school aid funds as part of our education program, improve the quality of teaching, training, and counseling in our hardest hit areas.

We must build more libraries in every area and more hospitals and nursing homes under the Hill-Burton Act, and train more nurses to staff them.

We must provide hospital insurance for our older citizens financed by every worker and his employer under Social Security, contributing no more than one dollar a month during the employee's working career to protect him in his old age in a dignified manner without cost to the Treasury, against the devastating hardship of prolonged or repeated illness.

We must, as a part of a revised housing and urban renewal program, give more help to those displaced by slum clearance, provide more housing for our poor and our elderly, and seek as our ultimate goal in our free enterprise system a decent home for every American family.

We must help obtain more modern mass transit within our communities as well as low-cost transportation between them.

Above all, we must release eleven billion dollars of tax reduction into the private spending stream to create new jobs and new markets in every area of this land.

My good friends and my fellow Americans: In these last seven sorrowful weeks, we have learned anew that nothing is so enduring as faith, and nothing is so degrading as hate.

John Kennedy was a victim of hate, but he was also a great builder of faith—faith in our fellow Americans, whatever their creed or their color or their station in life; faith in the future of man, whatever his divisions and differences.

This faith was echoed in all parts of the world. On every continent and in every land to which Mrs. Johnson and I traveled, we found faith and hope and love toward this land of America and toward our people.

So I ask you now in the Congress and in the country to

join with me in expressing and fulfilling that faith in working for a nation, a nation that is free from want and a world that is free from hate—a world of peace and justice, and freedom and abundance, for our time and for all time to come.

REAGAN ON POVERTY

The material that follows is taken from a speech by Ronald Reagan to the National Black Republican Council dinner

Remarks at a National Black Republican Council Dinner
September 15, 1982

Thank you very much. Mrs. Daniels, I thank you very much for those most generous words. Mr. Toastmaster, reverend clergy, the distinguished honorees and the ladies and gentlemen here at the head table, and you ladies and gentlemen:

It's a pleasure for Nancy and me to be here with you tonight. We know that you're in the forefront of one of the most important political battles of this election season, and we're with you heart and soul.

When it comes to improving the economic well-being and protecting the rights of all our citizens, our party doesn't play second-fiddle to anyone. When I entered office less than twenty months ago, we were in the midst of an economic catastrophe from which we're just now beginning to recover. All of us were suffering, especially the poor, the elderly, and the disadvantaged. Some of our political leaders were even saying that nothing could be done and that we had to accept a lower standard of living and that America's best days were behind us. Well, to those on the bottom of the economic ladder, that kind of talk is disaster. It robs them of hope and condemns them to a life of dependency and deprivation.

Our economic hardship is not some kind of mysterious malaise suffered by people who have suddenly lost their vitality. The problem is that the liberal economic policies that dominated America for too long just didn't work. It was not that those in power lacked good intentions; in fact, most of the compassionate rhetoric I mentioned a moment ago was not about accomplishments—it was about the wonderful intentions of the costly liberal programs. Well, too often the programs didn't do what they were supposed to and in many cases, they made things worse.

You know, they reminded me—those programs—and I've told this before, if you'll forgive me, and life not only begins at forty but so does lumbago and telling the same story [*Laughter*].

But they reminded me of that old story about the fellow riding the motorcycle on a chilled, cold winter day. The wind coming through the buttonholes in the front of the jacket was chilling him. So finally he stopped, turned the jacket around and put it on backward. Well, that protected him from the wind, but it kind of hindered his arm motion. And he hit a patch of ice and skidded into a tree. When the police got there, they elbowed their way through the crowd, and they said, "What happened?" They said, "We don't know." They said, "By the time we got his head turned around straight, he was dead." [*Laughter*]

The record is there for all to see. This country entered the 1960s having made tremendous strides in reducing poverty. From 1949 until just before the Great Society burst upon the scene in 1964, the percentage of American families living in poverty fell dramatically from nearly 33 percent to only 18 percent. True, the number of blacks living in poverty was still disproportionately high. But tremendous progress has been made.

With the coming of the Great Society, government began eating away at the underpinnings of the private enterprise system. The big taxers and big spenders in the Congress had started a binge that would slowly change the nature of our society and, even worse, it threatened the character of our people.

By the end of the decade, the situation seemed out of control. At a time when defense spending was decreasing in real dollars, the federal budget tripled. And, to pay for all of this spending, the tax load increased until it was breaking the backs of working people, destroying incentive, and siphoning off resources needed in the private sector to provide new jobs and opportunity.

Inflation had jumped to double-digit levels. Unemployment was climbing. And interest rates shot through the roof, reaching 21½ percent shortly before we took office. Perhaps the saddest part of the whole story is that much of this federal spending was done in the name of helping those it hurt the most, the disadvantaged. For the result of all that big spending and taxing is that, today, those at the lower end of the economic ladder are the hardest hit of all.

The decrease in poverty I referred to earlier started in the 1950s. By the time the full weight of Great Society programs was felt, economic progress for America's poor had come to a tragic halt. By 1980 the trend had reversed itself, and even more people, including more blacks, were living in poverty than back in 1969.

In 1980 the American people sent a message to Washington, D.C. They no longer believed that throwing tax money at a problem was acceptable, no matter how good the intentions of those doing the taxing and spending.

In 1980 the people turned to the Republican Party because we offered hope. Setting things straight would not be an easy job. Bringing back real growth to our economy and real increases in our standard of living would not be easy. But we Republicans knew it could be done, and we still know that. America's best days are not behind her, and we're moving forward to tackle the serious problems just as we said we would.

Our critics to the contrary, the poor and disadvantaged are better off today than if we had allowed runaway government spending, interest rates, and inflation to continue ravaging the American economy. A family of four, for example, on a fixed income of $15,000 would today be $833 poorer, that much weaker in purchasing power, if we hadn't brought inflation alone down as far as we have from the double-digit rates that we inherited. A similar family living at the poverty level would be $472 poorer if inflation had continued at the 12.4 percent rate. It's been 5.4 percent since January.

When one considers that the poor spend most of their family budgets on necessities—food, shelter, and clothing—leaving few ways to cut back to beat inflation, the importance of solving inflation is better understood.

We must remain firm and not be lured again into inflation-spending patterns. But let's be frank: The lives of those in the lower income levels are not what we'd like them to be. Some critics, especially in a political season, seem to forget that this administration didn't create the problem. The poverty and unemployment of today is the outgrowth of policies and problems of the late 1960s and the 1970s. Our program has just gone on line. And, if the current indicators are any suggestion, it's beginning to work.

WOMEN AND CHILDREN IN POVERTY

Hearing before the Task Force on Entitlements, Uncontrollables, and Indexing of the Committee on the Budget, House of Representatives, Ninety-eighth Congress, October 27, 1983

Statement of Kathy Baker, Annapolis, Md.

Ms. Baker. Good morning, Mr. Chairman and members of the committee. My name is Kathy Baker. I am the mother of three boys, ages ten, nine, and five, and I live in Annapolis, Maryland. I was raised in an upper middle-class family in Annapolis, where I attended parochial school, the Anne Arundel Community College, and a local business school. I had a stable family life and I never imagined that I would ever be "poor." Even further from my mind was the thought that my children would ever be without a father, without money, without a home.

During my nine-year marriage, my husband got involved with drugs and alcohol and became emotionally and physically abusive toward me and the children. As our family life deteriorated, I was faced with the decision of whether to stay in a destructive situation or leave so we could be safe. My husband's attacks became more violent and it got to the point where I was afraid for our lives. So in January 1982, in the middle of a snowstorm, the children and I sneaked out of the home we were renting and went to stay temporarily with some friends. I had no money, no home, no job, and three small children. There were three adults and seven children in that one home. We were crowded and the boys and I slept on the floor but it was the only place we could go at that time.

I had been in counseling at the YWCA's Women's Center so I called there for assistance in finding an attorney. I was given the names of several women lawyers and I picked a woman who turned out to be a dear friend as well as a caring attorney. She gave guidance and friendship and even hand-me-down clothes so I would have something to wear as I worked in her office in exchange for legal help. She told me to go to social services. About that time I was beginning to panic. I knew we could not live with friends forever, and my husband refused to support the children or even get a job. I desperately needed money, but welfare could not be the only answer for me.

As I realized that I was indeed a woman in poverty and my sons depended on me alone for everything, I began to do whatever was necessary to help us get out of this situation. I went to social services in a daze. It was a cold, impersonal place and the staff was unsmiling and un- touched by a situation they had seen countless times before. I was devastated—but to them, it was just one more person asking for money. As endless questions were asked, I began to feel like my integrity was doubted—like I was lying just to get the money. I even began to feel guilty for asking for aid. I was ready to walk out because it was too humiliating to go on. But we were in real need and my children deserved these benefits so I kept on.

Within three days or so, I received $161 in food stamps. I would receive that each month. I was told that in about one month, I would receive the AFDC grant. That is a long time to wait when you have nothing to live on. Our AFDC check was $385 per month. While I was grateful, what hit me immediately was that this would never be enough for rent, utilities, and nonfood items. I was scared. I had not worked outside the home in the nine years I had been a mother and a homemaker and I needed to settle my family in a home of our own. Our living situation had become impossible to continue. I was on the waiting list for public housing but I was told that would take about two years. Again. I was fortunate to have so many friends and family in the Annapolis area. None of them are wealthy, but I always had their support.

My parents fixed up their attic and the adjoining bedroom and we moved in with them and my sister and my brother in March 1982. Again, four adults and four children was crowded but necessary. I was immediately informed that my food stamps would be terminated, because I was living in my parents' home. My parents certainly could not afford to feed four extra people. I still needed the food stamps, and the only way I could continue receiving them was to set up separate cooking and food storage facilities in my bedroom. Those facilities were only an electric skillet and a hotplate.

I did not want to further burden my family so I began working part-time for my attorney. She started paying me instead of using our "barter" arrangement. When I told social services that I was working three days per week, I was told that I would lose all of the grant—but food stamps would continue at a decreased amount. Every time I took a step forward, I was pushed back a few steps. I did not see how I could ever get back on my feet, let alone ever get ahead of the game. A staff member at social services even suggested to me that I stay on welfare and forget about working as it would be easier. She said you have been doing fine since then, up until now. Why not just continue that way? But I did not want to stay on welfare forever—I just wanted some financial aid while I learned how to do my job so I could go on to earn more money and maybe even save a little money for emergencies. I did not want my children to grow up on welfare. Instead I wanted them to see me working to make myself a better person and to make a better life for them. It was discouraging and depressing being shoved back while I was struggling to go forward.

When I started working full time, medical assistance was also withdrawn and I had no health insurance for me and the children. Food stamps were dropped down to $25 per week. It was so frustrating. I paid some rent and utility payments to my parents; all miscellaneous items, doctor bills and medicine and a large portion of my paycheck went toward day care for my children. Yet, not one staff member at social services ever told me I could get free day care whenever I called to inform them of changes and pay increases with my job. I still could not afford rent for an apartment as I was told that with three children I would have to rent by law a three-bedroom unit, maybe even four bedrooms, and that would cost over four hundred dollars per month plus utilities. I was working full time yet going nowhere. A friend then told me about free day care. In December 1982 I was able to share a home with a divorced mother of two for three hundred dollars per month. It had then been almost one year since I had first gone to social services. The free day care is an excellent program and a very necessary one, yet it was never mentioned as a possible source of help to me. When I got it I was able to work while my children attended free day care—saving me about $365 a month It is the only benefit that was not taken away as I tried to advance.

I was so tired of always being told that I made too much money. I was "too poor" to make it on my own, but yet "too rich" to receive financial assistance—just some solid advice and support would have been welcome even if money were not available to me. I did not want to take advantage of the welfare programs, I just wanted some temporary help.

I would like to also mention here that even grocery shopping became an ordeal. Clerks have embarrassed me countless times I have been told to get a job. A ring that I was wearing, my great-grandmother's ring—I cannot sell something that is not mine, it is mine to care for and I wore it proudly—I cannot tell you how many people commented on that alone. If I dress well I am judged harshly. If I dress in jeans and a T-shirt I am judged harshly. In other words, why is she on welfare if she is dressed so nicely, but when I had on jeans and a T-shirt, it was why does she dress so sloppily.

My ex-husband's salary was finally garnished in May 1983. I had petitioned the court for child support and domestic relations had to go through their paperwork and other procedures before we began receiving payments of fifty dollars per week last May. A portion of his payments went to reimburse social services and the remainder went to the children. It was not enough to get us out of another unsuitable living situation, but just enough to wipe out my food stamps altogether. After only five months of receiving child support, it will now end since my ex-husband has left the state of Maryland. I will not be reapplying, however. I am fortunate enough to have met a man who wants to marry me and help me care and provide for my three children. But I often wonder—what if I had not met him? My situation was no different from what many women face. And it could happen to me again or to someone I care for. I worry about other women faced with these problems and setbacks who are not as fortunate as I have been. Only a very few women are so lucky, and I thank God I am one of the lucky ones.

Thank you.

SUMMARY OF THE ECONOMIC OPPORTUNITY ACT OF 1964

Fiscal 1965 Authorization: $947.5 Million

The Economic Opportunity Act of 1964 establishes an Office of Economic Opportunity in the Executive Office of the President. The OEO is headed by a director who has a planning and coordinating staff responsible for coordinating the poverty-related programs of all government agencies. Within the OEO, separate staffs operate a Job Corps, a program for Volunteers In Service To America (VISTA), a Community Action Program, and special programs for migrant workers. In addition, the OEO distributes funds to existing agencies to operate other programs authorized under the bill: work-training programs administered through the Labor Department; work-study programs and adult basic education through HEW (Department of Health, Education, and Welfare); special rural antipoverty programs through Agriculture; small business loans through the Small Business Administration; and community work and training projects for welfare recipients through HEW.

Following is a summary of the programs authorized under the Economic Opportunity Act of 1964:

Title I—Youth Programs: $412.5 million.

Part A–establishes a *Job Corps* to provide education, work experience, and vocational training in conservation camps and residential training centers; would enroll 40,000 young men and women, aged sixteen to twenty-one, this year, 100,000 next year. Administered by Office of Economic Opportunity. Total cost, $190 million.

Part B–establishes a *Work-Training Program* under which the Director of OEO enters into agreements with state and local governments or nonprofit organizations to pay part of the cost of full- or part-time employment to enable 200,000 young men and women, sixteen to twenty-one, to continue or resume their education or to increase their employability. Administered by Labor Department. Total cost, $150 million.

Part C–establishes a *Work-Study Program* under which the Director of OEO enters into agreements with institutions of higher learning to pay part of the costs of part-time employment to permit 140,000 students from low-income families to enter upon or continue higher education. It is administered by Department of Health.

Title II—Community Action Programs: $340 million.

Part A–authorizes the Director of OEO to pay up to 90 percent of the costs of antipoverty programs planned and carried out at the community level. Programs will be administered by the communities and will coordinate poverty-related programs of various federal agencies. Total cost, $315 million.

Part B–authorizes the Director to make grants to states to provide basic education and literacy training to adults. Administered by the Department of Health, Education, and Welfare. Total cost, $25 million.

Part C–authorizes the Director to establish and operate a clearinghouse to facilitate arrangements between foster parents willing to provide financial support and needy children under the guidance of a local agency. Only administrative funds required.

Title III—Programs to Combat Poverty in Rural Areas: $35 million.

Part A–authorizes loans up to $2,500 to very low-income rural families for farm operations and nonagricultural, income-producing enterprises, and loans to low-income family cooperatives. Administered by Department of Agriculture.

Part B–authorizes assistance to establish and operate housing, sanitation, education, and child day-care programs for migrant farm workers and their families. Total cost, not more than $15 million, financed from other Titles.

Part C–authorizes the Secretary of Agriculture to indemnify farmers whose milk has been polluted by pesticides recommended by USDA. No specific funds authorized.

Title IV—Employment and Investment Incentives

Authorizes loans and guarantees to small businesses of up to $25,000 on more liberal terms than the regular loan provisions of the Small Business Administration. Administered by the Small Business Administration. Would use SBA's regular spending authority.

Title V—Work-Experience Programs: $150 million.

Authorizes the Director of OEO to transfer funds to HEW to pay costs of experimental, pilot, or demonstration projects designed to stimulate the adoption in the states of programs of providing constructive work experience or training for unemployed fathers and needy persons.

Title VI—Administration and Coordination: $10 million.

Establishes the Office of Economic Opportunity and specifies its functions. Authorizes the Director of OEO to recruit and train an estimated five thousand VISTA volunteers to serve in specified mental health, migrant, Indian, and other federal programs including the Job Corps, as well as in state and community antipoverty programs.

Title VII—Treatment of Public Assistance

A policy declaration that an individual's opportunity to participate in programs under this Act shall neither jeopardize, nor be jeopardized by, his receipt of public assistance.

GLOSSARY

AFDC Aid to Families with Dependent Children: a provision of the Social Security Act of 1935 which provides assistance to families in which a dependent child is "deprived of parental support." When people speak of "welfare," they are generally thinking of AFDC.

anthropologist One who studies the characteristics and customs of cultures.

assumption Something taken for granted. An example is the assumption that stars will shine at night.

attitude A system of beliefs regarding some object and resulting in an evaluation of that object.

blaming the victim Concept invented by William Ryan in which the blame for a problem is placed on the victim.

cultural approach to poverty This approach emphasizes characteristics of the poor themselves—their values, attitudes, and behavior—in order to explain the existence of poverty. (Contrast with **situational approach.**)

culture of poverty Oscar Lewis' notion that a distinctive culture exists among the poor in industrialized societies and that it is passed on from generation to generation.

deindustrialization A shift in the occupational structure, resulting in fewer jobs in heavy industry.

functional analysis Analysis that assumes that poverty, or other social ills, serve some function for nonpoor members of society—otherwise, it would be eradicated.

heterogeneous Dissimilar. When we speak of a heterogeneous country, we mean one with citizens from diverse ethnic, racial, and cultural backgrounds.

homogeneous Composed of similar parts. A homogeneous country is one in which citizens are primarily from one ethnic, racial, or cultural stock.

ideology Beliefs, attitudes, and opinions which form a set. An important idea is that many beliefs are socially determined, so that if you are born into a rich family, you will probably develop a different set of ideas, or ideology, than if you are born into a poor family.

individualistic explanations of poverty   are explanations which look to characteristics of individuals in order to account for why they are poor. (Contrast with **structural explanations.**)

indoor relief   Forms of assistance to the poor which take place in public institutions, such as almshouses. An example is the institution portrayed in Charles Dickens' *Oliver Twist.*

internalization   Process whereby one assimilates the norms and values of parents and of society and makes them one's own.

laissez faire   Literally, "allow to act"; the theory that government should intervene as little as possible in the direction of economic affairs.

life chances   Probability that persons or groups will benefit from the opportunities available in a society. This varies according to race, class, ethnic group, etc.

outdoor relief   Poor relief that is provided directly to those being assisted, without their being lodged in institutions.

paradox   Something which does not make sense logically; a contradiction. Example: flying fish.

per capita income   Literally, "by heads"—the total income of a geographic area, divided by the number of people in the area.

policy   Course of action adopted to address a problem.

poverty line   A threshold set by the federal government, below which people are considered to be poor. The poverty line can be adjusted to take into account size of family, geographic location, and changes in the cost of living.

principle of less eligibility   Principle that the condition of all welfare recipients should be worse than that of the lowest-paid self-supporting laborer. This principle has been used to justify keeping welfare payments at a low level in several states.

research findings   Conclusions of a study, based on data collected.

situational approach to poverty   Approach to poverty which regards behavior of the poor as a response to particular features of the environment, as adaptations to specific situations. (Contrast with **cultural approach.**)

social costs   The negative effects of a social problem upon a society. These can be actively harmful, as in the case of crime or pollution, or they can involve the loss of a possible good, like the lack of productivity of an injured worker or the loss of the potential contributions of a high school dropout.

Social Darwinism   This doctrine has two central assumptions: (1) There are underlying forces in societies that are like forces in nature, and (2) These social forces elevate certain people and reduce others to poverty through the natural conflicts between social groups.

stereotype   A fixed picture, often based on ignorance or misinformation, of what is believed to be typical of a group. Example: White basketball players cannot jump high enough to excel in the sport.

structural explanations of poverty   look to aspects of the social structure or environment to account for the existence of poverty. (Contrast **individualistic explanations.**)

structural unemployment   Unemployment caused by changes in available jobs in particular sectors like manufacturing.

values   Beliefs held so deeply that one is willing to act upon them. These may be socially shared, so that one can speak of the values of a society.

work ethic   (sometimes called the **Protestant work ethic**). A concept in which the values of hard work, thrift, and deferred gratification are assumed to lead to worldly success, which is seen as a sign of God's favor.

workfare   An approach to relieving poverty in which the recipient of aid is expected to work in exchange for assistance.

working poor   Used to describe those who work for all or part of a year and still fall below the poverty line.

BIBLIOGRAPHY

Poverty

Auletta, Ken. *The Underclass*. New York: Random House, 1982.

Bagdikian, Ben H. *In the Midst of Plenty*. Boston: Beacon Press, 1964.

Beeghley, Leonard. *Living Poorly in America*. New York: Praeger, 1983.

Children's Defense Fund. *American Children in Poverty*. Washington, D.C.: Children's Defense Fund, 1984.

Danziger, Sheldon H., and Daniel H. Weinberg, eds. *Fighting Poverty: What Works and What Doesn't*. Cambridge, Mass.: Harvard University Press, 1986.

Edelman, Marian Wright. *Families in Peril: An Agenda for Social Change*. Cambridge, Mass.: Harvard University Press, 1987.

Feagin, Joe R. *Subordinating the Poor*. Englewood Cliffs, N.J.: Prentice Hall, 1975.

Harrington, Michael. *The New American Poverty*. New York: Holt, Rinehart and Winston, 1984.

Hopper, Kim, and Jill Hamberg. *The Making of America's Homeless: From Skid Row to New Poor*. New York: Community Service Society of New York, 1984.

Katz, Michael B. *Poverty and Policy in American History*. New York: Academic Press, 1983.

Lewis, Oscar. *The Children of Sanchez: Autobiography of a Mexican Family*. New York: Random House, 1961.

Marris, Peter. *Dilemmas of Social Reform: Poverty and Community Action in the United States* 2d ed. Chicago: University of Chicago Press, 1982.

Miller, William D. *Dorothy Day: A Biography*. San Francisco: Harper and Row, 1982.

Mority, Charles, ed. *Current Biography 1962* New York: H. W. Wilson Company, 1962.

Paglin, Morton. *Poverty and Transfers In-Kind: A Re-evaluation of Poverty in the United States.* Stanford, Calif.: Hoover Institution Press, Stanford University, 1980.

Rainwater, Lee. *Persistent and Transitory Poverty: A New Look.* Cambridge, Mass.: Joint Center for Urban Studies of MIT and Harvard University, 1981.

Rogers, Harrell R., Jr. *Poor Women, Poor Families: The Economic Plight of America's Female-Headed Households.* Armonk, N.Y.: M. E. Sharpe, 1986.

Ryan, William. *Blaming the Victim.* New York: Random, 1972.

Schiller, Bradley R. *The Economics of Poverty and Discrimination.* 4th ed. Englewood Cliffs, N.J.: Prentice Hall, 1984.

Stallard, Karin, Barbara Ehrenreich, and Holly Sklar. *Poverty in the American Dream: Women and Children First.* New York: Institute for New Communications: Boston: South End Press, 1983.

Waxman, Chaim Isaac. *The Stigma of Poverty: A Critique of Poverty Theories and Policies.* 2d ed. New York: Pergamon Press, 1983.

Public Welfare

Aaron, Henry H. *On Social Welfare.* Cambridge, Mass.: Abt Books, 1980.

Georges, Susan. *Ill Fares the Land: Essays on Food, Hunger, and Power.* Washington, D.C.: Institute for Policy Studies, 1984.

Goodwin, Leonard. *Do the Poor Want to Work?* Washington, D.C.: The Brookings Institution, 1972.

Katz, Michael B. *In the Shadow of the Poorhouse: A Social History of Welfare in America.* New York: Basic Books, 1986.

Levitan, Sar A. *Programs in Aid of the Poor for the 1980s.* 4th ed. Baltimore: Johns Hopkins University Press, 1980.

Patterson, James T. *America's Struggle Against Poverty, 1900–1980*. Cambridge, Mass.: Harvard University Press, 1981.

Sommers, Paul M., ed. *Welfare Reform in America: Perspectives and Prospects*. Boston: Kluwer-Nijhoff, 1982.

Trattner, Walter F. *From Poor Law to Welfare State: A History of Social Welfare in America*. 3d ed. New York: Free Press; London: Collier-MacMillan, 1984.

Hunger

Physician Task Force on Hunger in America. *Hunger in America: The Growing Epidemic*. Middletown, Conn.: Wesleyan University Press, 1985.

For Young Readers

Lens, Sidney. *Poverty: Yesterday and Today*. New York: Thomas Y. Crowell, 1973.

Liston, Robert A. *The American Poor: A Report on Poverty in the U.S.* New York: Delacorte Press, 1970.

The New Deal

Blumberg, Barbara. *The New Deal and the Unemployed: The View from NYC*. Lewisburg, Pa.: Bucknell University Press, 1979.

Davis, Kenneth Sydney. *FDR, the New Deal Years, 1933–1937: A History*. New York: Random House, 1986.

Leff, Mark Hugh. *The Limits of Symbolic Reform: The New Deal and Taxation, 1933–1939*. Cambridge, Cambridgeshire, England, and New York: Cambridge University Press, 1984.

Louchheim, Katie, ed. *The Making of the New Deal: The Insiders Speak*. Cambridge, Mass.: Harvard University Press, 1983. Contains historical notes by Jonathan Dembo.

Smith, Page. *Redeeming the Time: A People's History of the 1920s and the New Deal*. New York: McGraw-Hill, 1987.

Periodicals

N. Amidei. "Poverty 1965–1985." *Commonweal* 112 (6/21/85) 364–65.

V. Cahan. "The Feminization of Poverty: More Women Are Getting Poorer." *Business Week* (1/28/85) 84–85.

J. Conant. "Poverty: The War Isn't Over [Census Bureau Report]." *Newsweek* 106 (9/9/85).

Gregory A. Fossedal. "The Second War on Poverty." *American Spectator* 19 (February 1986) 14.

J. K. Galbraith. "How We Get the Poor Off Our Conscience." *Cent Magazine* 19 (May and June 1986).

D. Goddy. "A National Dilemma: Poverty Amid Plenty." *Scholastic Update* 117 (3/15/85) 21–22.

N. Lemann. "The Origins of the Underclass, Part 1." *Atlantic* 257 (6/86) 31–43.

N. Lemann. "The Origins of the Underclass, Part 2." *Atlantic* 258 (7/86) 54–68.

G. C. Loury. "The Family, The Nation, and Senator Moynihan." *Commentary* 81 (6/86) 21–26.

M. Magnet. "America's Underclass: What To Do?" *Fortune* 115 (May 11, 1987) 130–34.

E. Magnuson. "In Search of New Approaches [Democratic Conference on the Poor] *Time* 128 (7/7/86).

C. A. Murray. "Helping the Poor: A Few Modest Proposals." *Commentary* 79 (5/85) 27–34.

C. Murray and J. L. Jackson. "What Does the Government Owe the Poor?" *Harpers* 272 (4/86) 35–39.

R. P. Nathan. "Will the Underclass Always Be With Us?" *Society* 24 (March and April 1987) 57–62.

C. O'Connor. "Affluent America's Forgotten Children." *Newsweek* 107 (6/2/86) 20–21.

J. W. Skillen. [Views of C. A. Murray; with reply by J. Halteman and R. H. Nash] "In Search of Something That Works." *Christianity Today* 29 (6/14/86) 26–30.

D. Watkins-Hamilton. "Fighting Back." *Nation* 242 (1/18/86) 36–37.

INDEX